MW00803918

ZAHAV HOME

Cooking for Friends & Family

Michael SOLOMONOV
Steven COOK

ZAHAV HOME

Cooking for Friends & Family

Michael SOLOMONOV
Steven COOK

Produced by Dorothy Kalins Ink
Photography: Michael Persico
Art Direction: Don Morris Design
Recipe Editor: Kim O'Donnel

HARVEST
An Imprint of WILLIAM MORROW

Photography © 2024 by Michael Persico

Produced by Dorothy Kalins Ink, LLC

Art Direction by Don Morris Design

Recipe Editor: Kim O'Donnel

HarperCollins books may be purchased for educational, business, or sales promotional use. For information, please email the Special Markets Department at SPsales@harpercollins.com.

FIRST EDITION

Library of Congress Cataloging-in-Publication Data has been applied for.

ISBN 978-0-358-69736-7

24 25 26 27 28 IMG 10 9 8 7 6 5 4 3 2 1

Dedication

To our children, Noura, Danny, Eva, Lucas, David, Sally, and Leo:
Eat your vegetables!

Contents

CHAPTER 3

Chicken 116

CHAPTER 4

Vegetables 162

Contents

CHAPTER 7

Fish 294

CHAPTER 8

Desserts 318

Welcome!

Introduction

May 5, 2023. Zahav turned fifteen today. Although by the time you read this, the restaurant will be at least a year older. Fifteen years is an eternity in this business. When it opened in Philadelphia in 2008, Zahav was our third restaurant. Now we have more than twenty. Back then, our two families had one child between us. Now there are seven.

We thought the fact that we opened an Israeli restaurant on Cinco de Mayo might explain why we were so slow that first night. It did not.

It's easy to forget that Zahav was not always the landmark restaurant it is today. But those first six months were weighed down by the prospect of a very quick failure. Every restaurant business plan ends with James Beard Awards and cookbooks and television appearances and celebrity guests and restaurant empires. But fairy tales rarely come true. That it happened at Zahav is a gift we never take for granted.

"Why don't we do this every night?" asked Danny Cook, lining up for kebabs with David and Lucas Solomonov to his left, and twin sister Eva, right.

"We did the only thing that made us feel close to normal: We cooked." —*STEVE*

It helps to remember that our original office was in a windowless attic above the bathrooms, accessible by a pull-down ladder. That ladder blocked a hallway to the prep kitchen, frequently trapping us inside. In summertime, the heat was oppressive. We couldn't afford to throw anything away—we might need it again someday—so we watched as a tsunami of restaurant detritus occupied the attic. It was closing in on us.

After four years, we took over the space next to Zahav, a former recording studio, and added private rooms, kitchen space, and . . . a dedicated office. But still no windows. We had air-conditioning, but no heat. In the winter our fingers were so numb it was sometimes hard to type. But those of us who did time in the attic didn't complain.

A few years later, we rented a proper office in a proper office building in Center City. It even had a conference room and a kitchenette. We felt like grown-ups, at the helm of an exciting and growing business that now boasted eight brands and fourteen locations.

And then on March 16, 2020, everything stopped. In a matter of a few hours, we went from more than four hundred employees to zero employees. For all our experience managing the daily challenges of our business (not enough staff/too much staff, not enough customers/too many customers, power outages, ingredient shortages, broken equipment, bad reviews,

"So how do Zahav's signature ideas make the trip home?" —*MIKE*

red ink), nothing had prepared us for this moment. There was no precedent, no instruction manual, no move that would make a bit of difference in the face of a global pandemic.

And so, with no idea what else to do, we did the only thing that made us feel close to normal: We cooked.

We cooked breakfast and lunch for our families. And then we cooked dinner. In between, because we lived near each other then, we took laps around the park in our neighborhood. There was so much bad news. So much cause for pessimism.

Cooking and eating together was our salvation. It occupied our hands and our minds. And every once in a while, one of us would cook something that would startle us into saying: "This would be really good on the menu." A little glimpse of hope for the future.

As the weeks turned into months, and as we cooked our food at home, we grew convinced that these recipes could become a book. This book was born of that time: These recipes reflect the flavors of Zahav that have seeped into our veins (and our clothes) these last fifteen years.

But restaurant cooking is not home cooking—unless you happen to have a battery of trained chefs in your kitchen. And even then (because we *are* trained chefs) we needed to figure out how to bring the flavors of Zahav to our home kitchens without all that labor.

In other words, even though we know

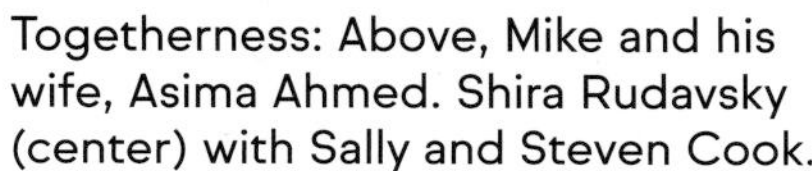

Togetherness: Above, Mike and his wife, Asima Ahmed. Shira Rudavsky (center) with Sally and Steven Cook.

how to do it, we don't always want to do it. Not every day is a Sunday. Some days are Tuesdays, and you get home after dark and the kids are melting down. And some days are Fridays when you will do almost anything to avoid washing dishes.

So how do Zahav's signature ideas make the trip home from the restaurant? The most obvious way is through a strategically stocked home pantry—which is why we put our Pantry section right at the front of this book. If you have these ingredients at your fingertips, it's nothing, for example, to slather amba from a jar onto a spatchcocked chicken for an almost-instant roast chicken dinner. And we figured out a leg of lamb coated with harissa (also from a jar!) made in one pot. On a school night!

As busy fathers—and cooks—we've learned to think ahead. When we make soups—and we do make them at home with all the intense flavors and complex ingredients we use at the restaurant—we make a lot of soup, always thinking of the freezer and of those late nights when there's no time to cook.

We've made our Salad and Vegetable chapters deliberately robust because these days, it seems veggies are what we want to eat. At the restaurant, its our job to work out complex flavors and serve them to you in surprising ways. But at home we crave simpler things like delightful Tehina Caesar Salad and even a Pittsburgh Wedge Salad with Labneh Ranch Dressing.

We transport the spirit of Zahav's mezze course to the home kitchen with recipes like Butternut Squash Baba Ganoush with Pomegranate Seeds & Pepitas, a knockout dinner party dish. We love our chraime, a North African spiced braise, and serve it often with fish at the restaurant. At home, we've developed a Cauliflower Chraime so flavorful it can be eaten hot or cold, over pasta, or when we're starving at 2 a.m.

But some days are Sundays, when there are no time constraints and cooking

> "Cooking is the best nonprescription anxiety treatment we know."—*STEVE*

becomes a meditation on the present, when getting dinner on the table on time is not really the main objective. These are the days to immerse yourself in the pleasures of cooking, to try out new ideas, and to take some risks. Our Eggplant T'bit (along with a few other recipes in this book) calls for flipping the finished dish upside down onto a serving platter while holding your breath as your guests ooh and aah. It may not always work out, but it sure is fun (and usually delicious).

We practiced what we preach in making this book. Our first book, *Zahav: A World of Israeli Cooking,* was made at the restaurant, with a battery of trained chefs bringing dishes at various stages of completion to be photographed.

In *Zahav Home,* we cooked every dish in Mike's kitchen, from scratch, in a single take. And we washed all the dishes. Many of the photographs in this book document the first time these recipes were ever made. And many of the recipes were improvised and improved on the spot, because after all, that's half the fun of cooking.

The other half is this: When we cook, we are literally nurturing ourselves and the people we love. It is an inherently generous act, the meaning of which should never be minimized.

Cooking is also the best nonprescription anxiety treatment we know. It sharpens our focus and quiets our minds. It is a window for reflection and contemplation. Most of our best ideas have occurred to us while cooking, and some of them are not even about food!

Sometimes we need to zoom out to appreciate what we have. When we're deep "in the weeds" (as we say when we're drowning in orders on a busy night), it's too easy to fixate on the negatives—bad reviews, difficult HR conversations, financial pressures—all the things that come with the territory when you're running a restaurant.

But looking back on fifteen years of Zahav, we can see we've been given an extraordinary gift: We've been able to pursue something we love, something that fills us with meaning, and we have been rewarded for it—critically, financially, and spiritually.

Conventional wisdom holds that when it comes to food, the pleasure is in the eating. But we believe context is everything. It's the difference between ordering in a meal from a virtual restaurant dropped off by a third-party delivery service and a meal served to you at your favorite neighborhood spot. It's the difference between dinner eaten in front of the television and one shared around a table of family and friends. It's the difference between a house and a home.

Our Kale Salad, page 64, is a rainbow: kale, pistachios, mandarin oranges, red onion, and jewel-like pomegranate seeds. Eva Cook, opposite.

ZAHAV MINI-5 SPICE SET

We entrust our spice program at the restaurant to our friend Lior Lev Sercarz of La Boîte in New York, so why should you settle for anything less? May we suggest this Zahav gateway sampler pack to begin your spice journey? It has classics like za'atar, baharat, and hawaij that we couldn't live without, along with some of Lior's proprietary blends inspired by his travels as a chef and spice merchant.

TEHINA

Our partnership with Soom Tahini, a Philly-based purveyor founded by three American sisters, is almost as old as Zahav itself. And for good reason. Tehina is so important to our cuisine that only the best will do. Made from 100 percent ground sesame seeds (the humera variety from Ethiopia), tehina is not just the not-so-secret ingredient in our hummus. We use it throughout our cooking as a sauce, dip, salad dressing, and dessert ingredient. Tehina's ability to add richness and creaminess to dishes without adding dairy makes it especially welcome in vegan and kosher kitchens.

BAHARAT

We affectionately refer to this spice blend as Turkish or Middle Eastern pumpkin pie spice due to its mix of sweet and savory. Baharat is not a single thing; the name translates from the Arabic word for "spices," and blends vary from region to region (and even house to house) throughout the Middle East.

Our favorite version is in the Arabic style and includes cinnamon, cloves, mace, nutmeg, and allspice, cut with a healthy dose of black pepper. A Turkish-style baharat, by contrast, would include more savory spices like cumin, paprika, and coriander, along with dried mint. Great with sweet things, we think baharat is at its best as a seasoning for meat and chicken, adding a distinctive Levantine note to kebabs, roast chicken, or stuffed vegetables. It's brilliant in rice pilaf. And of course it works in sweet applications as well. Add some to your favorite cocoa mix. Or bake a Middle Eastern pumpkin pie.

ZAHAV HOME
Pantry

Bringing Zahav home is not about mastering cheffy restaurant tricks. It's about replicating flavors. It's about assembling an inspired stash—a strategic collection of just the right herbs and condiments: the fragrant dried leaves and seeds; the aromatic pods and berries; the silky syrups and deeply pungent peppery pastes; the zesty pickles and spicy sauces; the mellow cheeses and toasty grains, all available from our favorite purveyors (see page 364). This is where the flavor lives.

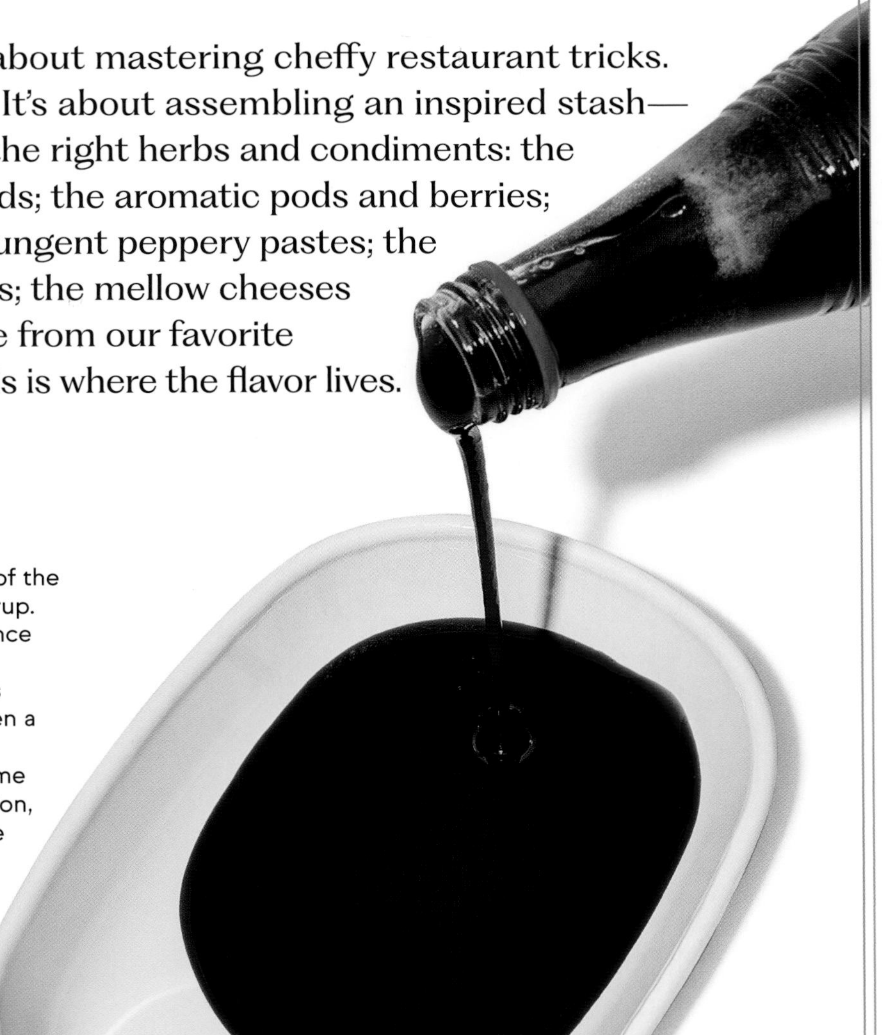

POMEGRANATE MOLASSES

Pomegranate molasses is simply the juice of the pomegranate cooked down into a thick syrup. It has a long shelf life and a signature balance of sweet and sour that makes it incredibly versatile in our pantry. The pomegranate is native to the Middle East and has long been a revered symbol. Today, it's considered an antioxidant superfood and shows up in some of the most well-known recipes of the region, like the Persian fesenjān and the Levantine dishes fattoush and muhammara. And of course, pomegranate molasses is a key ingredient in Zahav's world-famous lamb shoulder, so we've run through a truckload over the last fifteen years. But it can do so much more.

Pomegranate molasses is terrific in salad dressings instead of vinegar, in all kinds of stews, drizzled over roasted vegetables (or vanilla ice cream), in cocktails (grenadine is made from pomegranates), as a glaze for salmon, in barbecue sauce, or even to brighten up a fruit salad.

SMOKED PAPRIKA

For most of our lives, paprika lived in the dark corner of the spice cabinet, more food coloring than flavor. As culinary professionals, we met a whole new world of paprika. Smoked paprika's depth of flavor is our secret weapon, improving everything from eggs and potatoes to chicken. Our favorite is the Spanish pimentón de La Vera, so famous its quality is government-regulated. In La Vera, peppers are smoked over oak fires, dried, then slowly stone-milled to preserve color and flavor. Hungarian paprika is typically not smoked, but Hungarians take their paprika seriously and the quality is exceptional. Both Spanish and Hungarian paprikas come in sweet, smoky, and hot versions.

SMOKED CINNAMON

Imagine if every dish you cooked with cinnamon turned out just a little bit better. That's smoked cinnamon! Considered a baking spice, cinnamon does remarkable things to savory foods, too. The smoked version works both sides of the aisle, with a bit more complexity and flair than its sweet sister. We love cooking freekah with smoked cinnamon, adding it to kebabs, and seasoning lentil soup with it. It's the spice you didn't know was missing from your chili! And, of course, smoked cinnamon was one of our original Federal Donuts flavors, so you know it makes dynamite French toast.

BULGARIAN FETA

We're not supposed to call this feta, which is the exclusive dominion of Greece; but with apologies to the European Union, we all know what this really is. If you want to be polite, call it Bulgarian cheese like they do in Israel—just don't expect your cheesemonger to know what you're talking about!

The Bulgarian style of this brined, sheep's-milk cheese is creamier than the drier, crumblier authentic Greek feta. We love it so much, it's almost always somewhere on the menu at Zahav. It's the perfect finishing touch to punch up any number of vegetable dishes. We also love to eat it out of hand with olives, or in the classic Bulgarian style, with fat wedges of juicy watermelon in the summertime.

WHOLE WHEAT BERRIES

Wheat berries, the entire edible part of the wheat kernel (including bran, germ, and endosperm), are a delightful addition to your grain repertoire. We love their nutty flavor and pleasing chew. Wheat berries are a low-glycemic food—high in fiber and protein and other health benefits. Wheat berries are often confused with farro and spelt, which are other whole-grain wheat varieties. They are all delicious and we use them interchangeably in recipes. Wheat berries are terrific as the base for any grain salad or grain bowl. We particularly like them in long-cooked stews (like Beef Hamin, page 286) because they retain their bite when fully cooked without getting mushy.

For more on our favorite super grains, like beluga lentils, freekah, jasmine rice, chickpeas, Israeli couscous, bulghur, farro, and pearl barley, see Our Grain Pantry (page 260).

AMBA

Amba is a fermented mango condiment that was brought to Israel by Iraqi immigrants in the 1950s. Spiced with fenugreek, turmeric, and chiles, it's like Indian mango chutney ("amba" is the Marathi word for "mango"). This connection is said to reflect the presence of an influential Iraqi-Jewish community based in Mumbai in the nineteenth century. Amba is a defining ingredient in sabich—fried eggplant and hard-boiled eggs stuffed inside a pita—that has become a new Israeli classic.

We believe a little amba adds depth and complexity to tomato or barbecue sauce and excels brushed on grilled fish and as part of a marinade for chicken before roasting. Amba is powerful stuff (the fenugreek has a long half-life), so a little goes a long way. We especially like to whisk a small amount of amba into tehina sauce to carry the flavor without overpowering a dish.

BLACK LIME POWDER

The ground version of black lime can be more convenient to use, although the flavor dissipates much faster than its whole form, so you'll want to make sure you're buying the powder from a reputable source (meaning it hasn't sat for years) and using it relatively quickly. You can make your own black lime powder by blitzing whole dried black limes in a food processor and then sifting it. Black limes can also be grated on a Microplane, but you may want to skip your upper-body workout that week. Black lime powder is often used to season fish and is a common ingredient in Persian Gulf–style baharat blends. A small amount can add complexity to citrus-based drinks and desserts, like lemonade or Black Lime Bars (page 334). It can also be used as an herbal tea that is said to soothe indigestion.

CUCUMBER PICKLES

Canned, lacto-fermented pickles from Israel are one of our favorite treats. They are either sold as "Cucumbers in Brine" or "Cucumbers in Vinegar." These adorable finger-size cukes are fermented in brine in open vats in the sun. These are full-sour, in-your-face pickles, often with the addition of garlic. We've been known to eat a whole can in one sitting. These pickles are customarily served along with salatim to begin a meal in Israel and are a staple on falafel bars. They also go great with a corned beef sandwich.

BLACK LIMES

Fresh green limes—blanched in salted water and left to dry in the sun until they turn hard—become black limes! Sometimes referred to as limu omani because they were first produced in Oman, black limes are an important ingredient in the cuisines of Iran, Iraq, and other Persian Gulf countries (and, strategically, in ours, too). Black limes have a sour, salty flavor—not unlike sumac but with strong citrus notes—and a somewhat funky edge. In their whole form, they are often pierced with a knife and dropped into soups and stews, where their sour, fruity, and fermented notes add complexity and brightness to long-cooked dishes.

CORIANDER SEEDS

Coriander seeds are the dried fruit of the cilantro plant. The seeds have a floral, citrusy flavor with notes of orange. Coriander seeds, along with orange peels, are a traditional addition to many Belgian-style wheat beers, and an important botanical in flavoring gin (and Coca-Cola). Culinarily, crushed coriander seeds are a typical ingredient in garam masalas and Indian curries. In the Israeli kitchen, they are key to the North African spice blend we love (we call it the "Three C's": caraway, cumin, and coriander) and one of two must-have schug spices (along with cardamom).

One of our favorite uses for coriander seeds is in a version of tahdig, the crispy rice at the bottom of a pot of Persian rice. In this particular preparation, the bottom of the pot is lined with thinly sliced potatoes and scattered with coriander seeds. When the finished dish is inverted onto a serving platter, the top layer is a mosaic of golden brown potatoes and crunchy coriander seeds.

SILAN DATE SYRUP

Silan, aka date molasses, date syrup, or date honey, is made by pressing dates with water to yield a thick, glossy syrup. Biblical references to Israel as the "Land of Milk and Honey" are thought to refer to date molasses as the "Honey" in that equation. (Some brands include added sugar and are to be avoided.) The real deal has a nice amount of acidity to balance its sweetness. Like other fruit molasses, silan can be used in place of other sweeteners in baked goods. Another classic application involves drizzling silan over a piece of bread slathered with tehina. We use it with Urfa peppers in our glaze for chicken wings and brush it on the skin of grilled salmon. We like silan in beverages as well—try a spoonful stirred into a glass of milk.

TUNISIAN-STYLE LEMONS

Preserved lemons are a staple of North African cuisine, where they bring an intensely aromatic and complex citrus flavor to tagines, couscous, and salads. They are available in jars already cured, but we like to preserve our own, too. To make preserved lemons, slits are cut into the fresh fruit and the openings are packed with salt (and sometimes sugar and other spices). The salt leaches the juice from the lemons, which forms a brine that keeps them submerged for their long ferment.

Preserved lemons can last from a few weeks to up to a few months. When the lemons have cured (i.e., when we run out of patience), we remove the flesh and pith and thinly slice the tender rinds and use them to season a variety of dishes. Consider using preserved lemons in any recipe that calls for fresh lemon.

DRIED ZA'ATAR

Za'atar refers to a spice blend as well as to the native herb that is the basis for this blend. The herb is similar to oregano or marjoram, both of which can be substituted in a pinch. The za'atar spice blend also contains toasted sesame seeds, ground sumac, and salt. Za'atar is as much a fixture on the Levantine table as salt and pepper is on the American table. Pita dipped in olive oil and then za'atar is a common use, as is manakeesh—za'atar mixed with olive oil and spread on flat bread dough before baking. Labneh with za'atar and olive oil is a popular breakfast dish.

We love za'atar generously sprinkled over chopped salad or hummus, slathered on roast chicken, and rubbed on lamb chops. Look for bright green za'atar, which is a sign of freshness and quality, as well as an indication that the blend has not been stretched with fillers.

GROUND SUMAC BERRIES

Sumac was an important source of sour flavoring in the Middle East before lemons became widely available. It is a staple ingredient in the spice blend za'atar. We like to use sumac to bring acidity to dishes without adding liquid. It has a naturally salty taste (but contains no salt) and is sometimes used as a salt substitute. We like to sprinkle sumac liberally on salads and steamed vegetables to give an extra punch of flavor to finished dishes. We marinate thinly sliced onions with salt, sumac, and vinegar as an accompaniment and use it to season roast chicken. There is a lot of old, inert sumac on our shelves; for a fresh batch, look for berries that are more red than brown and appear a bit oily.

SHIPKA PEPPERS

We can't get enough of these spicy, pickled peppers, which are also known as Bulgarian carrot peppers for their orange color when fresh. These peppers were likely smuggled into Israel by European immigrants from behind the Iron Curtain. Like gremlins, shipka peppers are adorable, but don't be fooled: Shipkas pack a punch significantly spicier than jalapeños and even serrano peppers. We use their heat and acidity as a nice foil for rich foods like kebabs, shawarma, and falafel and other fried things. We slice them thinly in salads and sandwiches and scatter them over raw fish.

URFA PEPPER

Urfa biber ("pepper" in Turkish) is actually a sun-dried Turkish chile. Partway through drying, the peppers are sealed in plastic in a process called "sweating," which helps preserve some of their natural oils and gives them their trademark smoky, raisiny flavor as well as their deep purple-red color.

Urfa peppers are sold ground and are not terribly hot, which means you can use them generously, sprinkled over roasted potatoes, cauliflower, or carrots. They add earthy, chocolaty notes to long-cooked dishes and are terrific mixed with date molasses as a sweet and spicy glaze for chicken wings.

CARDAMOM

This powerful pod packs a fragrant punch with a piney, almost minty flavor. Native to Asia, cardamom traveled the legendary spice routes and was prized as a digestive aid. Ground cardamom is what gives our Yemenite latte at K'Far its trademark flavor, and it's one of the spices that makes schug so distinctive. We typically use the seeds of the green cardamom pod. Black cardamom is a related species with a distinctly smoky flavor.

HAWAIJ

"Hawaij" is an Arabic word that refers to a spice blend. Much like the term "curry," it doesn't mean just one thing. For example, there's a coffee hawaij with sweet spices like clove, cardamom, ginger, and cinnamon. And then there's the hawaij that we go to most often—a savory blend of cumin, black pepper, and turmeric—that is the hallmark of Yemenite soup. One trick we've developed over the years is to add the hawaij in two stages. First, at the beginning of cooking, to bloom the spices and provide a steady bass line to the dish. Then we finish the dish with more hawaij to add brightness and aroma.

CAROB MOLASSES

Carob molasses is made by cooking the fruit of the carob pod in water and then reducing the liquid into a sweet, viscous syrup. Native to the Eastern Mediterranean, carob (and carob molasses) was particularly valuable as a sweetener prior to the arrival of refined sugar to the region. The carob seed was also used as a standard measure of weight in the ancient gold trade (it is the origin of the word "carat"). The flavor of carob molasses is nicely balanced between chocolaty and fruity and can be used in a wide variety of ways: in baked goods, mixed with tehina as a dip for breads, in long braises, or as a glaze for grilled or roasted meat.

LABNEH

Labneh is strained Arabic-style yogurt (think Greek yogurt, only thicker, like a fresh, creamy cheese). Not surprisingly, strained yogurt as a means of preserving milk is part of many culinary traditions throughout the world, and labneh is a workhorse in the Levantine kitchen. Perhaps the best way to eat labneh is also the simplest—drizzled with good olive oil, dusted with za'atar, and scooped up with good bread. You can swap labneh for yogurt or sour cream in most recipes for a thicker, richer result. It's great as a base for dips—see French Onion Labneh (page 34), or Labneh Tzatziki & Grapes (page 311)—or in salad dressings like Labneh Ranch (page 42).

One of our favorite things to serve at parties is labneh balls rolled in spices and marinated in olive oil (page 26). Consider using labneh instead of yogurt in your morning parfait with fruit and granola, and as the star ingredient in cheesecake.

HARISSA

This fiery North African chile paste is a staple in the Maghreb (northwest Africa, including Morocco, Algeria, Tunisia, and Libya). As a pungent flavor base, harissa is used liberally in soups, tagines, and couscous, as a rub for meats and vegetables, and as a key ingredient in shakshuka. Harissa is so important to Tunisian cuisine that it has been designated part of the nation's Intangible Cultural Heritage by UNESCO. The seeds for the creation of harissa (pun intended) likely date back to the Spanish occupation of Tunisia in the sixteenth century, when New World products (like peppers) were proliferating around the globe.

What we love most about harissa is that it brings so much more than just heat to the table. The magical Maghrebi spice trio of caraway, cumin, and coriander adds dimension and intrigue to the peppery base in so many signature dishes. While harissa is easy to make at home, there are excellent jarred versions on the market, which we've put to good use in this book.

1

"My mom used to make carrot raisin salad with mayo all the time. I got over my aversion to mayo. Mike never did!"—*STEVE*

Salads

Chopped Salad with Labneh

Makes 4 servings

Like the devil, this salad goes by many names (but unlike the devil, it's actually good for you). Throughout the Levant it is known as Arabic, Shopska (Bulgarian), Ottoman, Palestinian, Lebanese, or Israeli salad. Whatever it's called, we can't get enough of it. There is scarcely a meal in Israel without this salad. The swoosh of labneh enriches the dish and creates a well to trap the delicious vegetable juices. Eat Chopped Salad with a chavita (omelet) for breakfast and you might just live forever (without selling your soul).

> "I love a citrus squeezer! It gets whatever juice there is to be gotten." —*MIKE*

- 4 Persian cucumbers (or 1 English cucumber)
- 2 medium bell peppers, chopped
- 1 pint cherry or grape tomatoes, halved or quartered, depending on size
- ½ medium red onion, finely chopped
- 1 cup stemmed and finely chopped parsley
- Juice of 1½ large lemons, plus more to taste
- 1½ teaspoons salt, plus more to taste
- 2 cups homemade Labneh (see METHOD, page 30), or one 16-ounce container
- Olive oil and za'atar, for garnish

• Slice the cucumbers in half lengthwise, then into quarters. Cut each quarter into strips about ½ inch thick, then cut the strips into ½-inch pieces.

• Transfer to a large bowl, then follow with the peppers, tomatoes, onion, and parsley. Resist the urge to mix between additions.

• Add the lemon juice and salt. Now toss all together until evenly mixed, letting the vegetables soften in the lemon juice. Taste for salt and acidity, adding more of each as needed.

• To serve: Swoosh about 3 generous spoonfuls of labneh in the middle of a platter, spreading it with the back of a big spoon to form a well in the middle. Spoon the vegetables into the center. Drizzle with olive oil and sprinkle with za'atar.

Making: Chopped Salad with Labneh

Persian cucumbers, like cherry tomatoes, are products of advanced Israeli agronomy. The cukes were developed in Northern Israel and are known there as Beit Alpha cucumbers. We like to cut the onion and the parsley extra fine so that they become a part of the dressing for the other vegetables.

"Chopped Salad is very forgiving. There are a million ways to make it."—*STEVE*

"Dress the salad right before serving to preserve the freshness of the vegetables."*—MIKE*

Marinated Labneh Balls

Makes about 18 pieces

(With a store-bought pint of labneh, drained, the yield will increase.)

This is an elegant way to dress up something as pedestrian-sounding as strained yogurt. And because the labneh balls keep so well in the fridge, we aspire to have a batch on hand in case an unexpected cocktail party breaks out. The balls never last that long, but fortunately, they're incredibly simple to make. Even if you've made the labneh, it may need to drain a bit. Roll the balls in one of any number of herbs, spices, nuts, or seeds. Za'atar is a classic and unbeatable partner. For a special treat, roll the balls in fruity Aleppo pepper and slather them on crusty bread with a drizzle of honey.

> "In the restaurant, we use a small ice cream scoop to make the balls. It goes faster." —*MIKE*

2 cups homemade Labneh (see METHOD, page 30), or one 16-ounce container, drained

Olive oil

FLAVORS

½ cup za'atar (or other dried herbs)

½ cup Aleppo pepper

For plain balls:
1 garlic clove, smashed, and a handful of dill sprigs

- In the palms of your hands, roll small bits of the labneh into teaspoon-size balls and arrange them on a plate.
- Coat the bottom of two or three small baking dishes with oil, and use separate bowls for each spice/flavor.
- Gently toss each of the balls into the spice mix of your choice. For plain balls, transfer directly to a prepared baking dish and add garlic and dill.
- Top with enough oil so the balls are partially submerged.
- Cover and marinate for 24 hours in the refrigerator. Marinated balls will keep well if they're totally submerged in olive oil.
- When ready to serve, bring the balls to room temperature. Smear on a bagel, toast, or a cracker, or just eat out of hand.

Making: Marinated Labneh Balls

"Labneh's easy to make—it just needs yogurt, salt, and time."—*STEVE*

Roll a spoonful of labneh between the palms of your hands to form a ball. Then roll the balls in Aleppo pepper or za'atar, or keep them plain. The balls luxuriate in a bath of olive oil until you're ready to use them. This enriches them and preserves their shape—and you can reuse the oil!

Love That Labneh

We love Loveneh labneh, handcrafted by Emiliano Tatar, a physician with a passion for making small-batch cave-aged cheese. And labneh.

Dr. Tatar and his wife, Lori Schwartz-Tatar, also a physician (and their two children, Mia and Seth), run Merion Park Cheese Co. from their home just outside Philly. Loveneh is made from organic milk that comes from Erivan Dairy (their yogurt is available in stores), an Armenian family farm in nearby Bucks County. Find Loveneh at merionparkcheese.com.

Method: Labneh

Makes about 1⅛ cups

It's quite satisfying (and easy) to transform yogurt into cheese—and also to use cheesecloth for its intended purpose. The hardest part is setting up the apparatus to suspend the cheese while the whey drains away. We like to save the rubber bands from bunches of supermarket vegetables and use them to secure the bundle of labneh to its rigging.

- 1 quart plain whole-milk, full-fat yogurt
- 2 tablespoons salt

• In a medium bowl, stir together the yogurt and salt.

• Nest a colander in a large bowl, then line the colander with four layers of cheesecloth.

• Pour the salted yogurt into the center of the cheesecloth, then gather all four corners of the cheesecloth to form a bundle. Tie into a knot, then twist to tighten. A rubber band will help secure it.

• Or make a sling: Tie the cheesecloth into a knot slung over the handle of a wooden spoon. Suspend the spoon over a bowl or colander.

• Refrigerate and let drain for several hours or overnight. Reserve the whey for another purpose. (It's great in Labneh Ranch Dressing, page 42.)

• Loosen the cheesecloth bundle. Labneh should be damp but not crumbly. It's ready to eat as is. (Or make Marinated Labneh Balls, page 26.)

• With a rubber spatula, scoop the drained labneh into an airtight container and store in the fridge, where it will keep for several weeks.

French Onion Labneh

Makes 4 generous servings

In the restaurant, adding the term "French Onion" to the name of any menu item instantly makes it sell like crazy. And for good reason. The deep, savory sweetness of properly caramelized onions combined with the tangy richness of dairy and a liberal amount of fresh herbs is a literal recipe for success. And labneh makes a lot of sense here, replacing the traditional mayonnaise with something lighter but no less decadent.

- 1 recipe Caramelized Onions (see METHOD, page 38), finely chopped
- 2 cups homemade Labneh (see METHOD, page 30), or one 16-ounce container
- ½ medium red onion, finely chopped
- ½ cup finely chopped chives
- ½ cup finely chopped dill
- 1 teaspoon salt, plus more to taste
- ½ teaspoon ground black pepper
- Juice of ½ lemon, plus more to taste

• Put everything but the lemon juice into a medium bowl. Stir together until evenly mixed, then add the lemon juice. Taste for lemon and salt, adding more as needed.

French Onion Labneh is the perfect anchor for a crudités platter, and it's often our go-to when we're staring down a pile of farm share vegetables that just keep coming, like in *Terminator 2*.

But let's be honest—we're really just thinking about potato chips right now.

METHOD

Caramelized Onions

Makes about ¾ cup

We've found that onions caramelize better when they're thinly sliced (as opposed to diced) since there's more surface area exposed to the pan. Salting at the end of the process also helps moderate the release of moisture from the onions for more consistent results. Just remember: low and slow. This process should not be rushed. Depending on your stove, it can take up to two hours.

"There's nothing like cooking to make you realize you don't know a GD thing about your life's work!" —*MIKE*

Olive oil

2 large onions, halved and cut into thin half-moons

- Coat the bottom of a 9- or 10-inch skillet with olive oil. Place the onions on top.
- Set the pan over high heat and leave it alone for a few minutes.
- Reduce the heat to medium-low and stir occasionally just to minimize sticking. Cook until the onions are soft and very well done—browned but not burned—adjusting the heat as needed. This process takes longer than you think it should! Cool before adding to the labneh, or cover and refrigerate. Caramelized onions can be frozen for a few months.

Pittsburgh Wedge Salad
with Labneh Ranch Dressing

Makes 4 servings

When attempting to get children to eat salad, we know french fries can be a powerful incentive. This is apparently true for all citizens of Pittsburgh, our hometown and adopted hometown, respectively. For in the great city of Pittsburgh, ketchup means Heinz, and salad means french fries, grated cheese, and iceberg lettuce. And meat. Our version is slightly more restrained: meat-free, with oven-roasted potatoes instead of deep-fried. Styled as a wedge salad and draped in Labneh Ranch Dressing, it cuts a very appealing figure for picky eaters of all ages. Yinz got it?

- 8 small Yukon potatoes, cut into steak fry wedges, about 1 inch thick
- 1 cup pickle juice from a can of shipka peppers, or your favorite pickle juice
- ¼ cup neutral oil, such as canola
- Salt, for seasoning
- 1 head iceberg lettuce, quartered into wedges
- 2 cups Labneh Ranch Dressing (see METHOD, page 42)
- 1 cup cherry tomatoes, halved
- ½ medium red onion, sliced into half-moons
- ½ to 1 cup grated cheddar cheese

- Marinate the potato wedges in a large bowl with the pickle juice and enough cold water to cover. Let marinate for at least 1 hour.
- Preheat the oven to 425°F.
- Drain the potatoes and transfer them to a sheet pan.
- Pour the oil over the potatoes, turning them until evenly coated. Arrange in a single layer, cut side down.
- Bake for 15 minutes. Turn the wedges onto the second side. Bake for an additional 10 minutes. Set the oven to the broiler setting and broil the potatoes until evenly brown, about 3 minutes. Sprinkle with salt.
- To serve: Set each lettuce wedge upright onto a plate.
- Ladle some dressing atop each wedge. Arrange a handful of tomato halves around each wedge, along with a few slices of onion.
- Perch a handful of potato wedges on top. Finish with grated cheddar.

METHOD

Labneh Ranch Dressing

Makes about 2 cups

A ranch dressing for the mayonnaise-phobes in your life.

- 1 cup homemade Labneh (see METHOD, page 30), or one 8-ounce container
- ½ cup stemmed and finely chopped parsley
- ½ cup stemmed and finely chopped dill
- ½ cup finely chopped chives
- 1½ teaspoons onion powder
- 1½ teaspoons garlic powder
- ½ teaspoon salt
- ½ teaspoon ground black pepper
- ¼ cup labneh whey, buttermilk, or lemon juice

• In a medium bowl, whisk together the labneh, parsley, dill, and chives. Add the onion powder, garlic powder, salt, and black pepper, stirring until evenly mixed. Stir in the whey. Taste for acidity (it should be a bit tart), adding a squeeze of lemon if needed.

Beets with Beet Greens Tzatziki

Makes 4 generous servings

Tzatziki is a yogurt-based sauce with Turkish and Greek origins, sometimes known as tarator. The name translates to "everything green," and the sauce usually includes cucumbers and fresh herbs. We love the idea of using up the greens that come free with many beet purchases (if your beets are greens-less, Swiss chard is a great substitute). The greens and their stems, cooked down with olive oil and garlic, make this tzatziki earthier and substantial enough to eat on its own.

- 4 medium beets (1½ to 2 pounds), thoroughly washed, greens reserved
- ½ cup apple cider vinegar
- 2 tablespoons salt, plus more for seasoning
- ¼ cup olive oil, plus more for finishing
- 4 garlic cloves, thinly sliced
- ½ large onion, cut into thin half-moons
- 2 Persian cucumbers, diced
- 2 cups homemade Labneh (see METHOD, page 30), or one 16-ounce container

• Cover the beets with cold water in a medium pot. Add the vinegar and salt. Over high heat, bring to a boil. Cover and reduce the heat to medium. Cook until a paring knife pierces them easily, about 1 hour. Remove and cool completely. If making in advance, cover and store in the refrigerator.

• When you're ready to cook the beet greens, rehydrate them in cold water for at least 10 minutes.

• Separate the beet stems from the leaves. Dice the stems and stack the leaves, roll them up tightly, and slice into a chiffonade, ribbon-shaped strips.

• Set a large skillet over medium heat and coat the bottom with olive oil.

• Add the garlic, onion, and stems, cooking until slightly softened, about 3 minutes. Stir in the leaves and cook until tender and visibly reduced, about 5 minutes.

• Remove from the heat and let cool. Finely chop and place in a bowl large enough to mix the tzatziki sauce.

• Add the cucumbers and the labneh, stirring until evenly mixed. Add salt to taste.

• Peel the beets and cut into wedges.

• To serve, spoon the tzatziki onto a platter. Center the beet wedges into a "rose." Finish with a drizzle of olive oil.

Making: Beets with Beet Greens Tzatziki

"If you boil your beets with about a half cup of apple cider vinegar, they'll lightly pickle as they cook." —*MIKE*

Once the beets are cooked and cooled, the skins will slip right off with a gentle rub. We like to use paper towels for this to keep our hands and all our kitchen towels from turning pink.

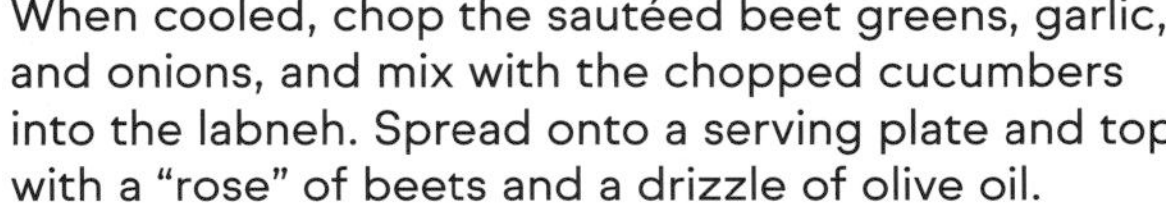

When cooled, chop the sautéed beet greens, garlic, and onions, and mix with the chopped cucumbers into the labneh. Spread onto a serving plate and top with a "rose" of beets and a drizzle of olive oil.

Heirloom Tomato Salad
with Shipka Peppers, Dill & Crispy Garlic

Makes 4 generous servings

We love having this salad in our repertoire for that time of year when tomatoes are good enough to live up to our expectations of them. Copious amounts of dill stand in admirably for the usual basil. The hot garlic oil amps up the already substantial umami from the tomatoes and creates a very cool temperature contrast. The juices that accumulate at the bottom of this salad are so good you might want to drink them.

- 1½ pounds heirloom tomatoes (or cherry tomatoes)
- Salt, for seasoning
- 2 or 3 shipka peppers, depending on size and degree of spiciness, plus some juice from the can
- 1 scant cup dill, washed and dried
- ½ cup Crispy Garlic (see METHOD, page 51)

• Cut the tomatoes into wedges and arrange on a large plate or platter. Season liberally with salt.

• Finely chop the peppers and scatter on top of the tomatoes. Spoon on some juice from the can, too.

• Remove the stems from the dill and discard. Coarsely chop the dill and scatter on top of the tomatoes.

• Spoon the oil from the Crispy Garlic, while still warm, over the dill (the garlic oil "cooks" the dill!). Top with the Crispy Garlic.

> "The last-second addition of hot garlic oil is a complete show biz experience. Everyone loves a tableside presentation!" —*MIKE*

Making: Heirloom Tomato Salad

Shipkas are a spicy Bulgarian chile that arrive canned in an acidic brine. Think of them as the peperoncini of Israel—thinly sliced and scattered, they add the perfect zing to anything from salad to pizza. Try a spoonful of the brine in your next Bloody Mary.

METHOD

Crispy Garlic

Makes ½ cup

This simple technique might change the way you think about garlic. And the oil's not bad either.

- ½ cup olive oil
- 4 garlic cloves, very thinly sliced

- When you're almost ready to dress the salad, pour the olive oil into a small saucepan.
- Add the garlic. Listen to the moisture popping!
- Cook over high heat until the garlic is golden in color and the oil is bubbling, about 3 minutes.
- Remove from the heat and stir the oil to cool it down.

Spinach Salad
with Watermelon, Feta & Olives

Makes 4 servings

This salad combines the ubiquitous Bulgarian-cum-Israeli combination of watermelon and feta with the fancy spinach salads of our youth ("fancy" meaning any greens other than iceberg lettuce). Many people will say that canned black olives have no flavor whatsoever. Nonsense. They taste like canned black olives, which is the taste of our childhood. If your childhood tasted like a different type of olive, by all means, use that one.

> **"We both grew up on canned olives, and we know they get a bad rap, but they're buttery and warm."** —*STEVE*

- ½ red onion, thinly sliced into half-moons
- 2 tablespoons red wine vinegar, plus more to taste
- ½ to 1 teaspoon dried and/or minced fresh mint, plus more to taste
- 1 4-pound seedless watermelon, sliced 1 inch thick
- ½ 6-ounce can black olives, drained (snack on the rest while you work!)
- 1 pound spinach leaves, thoroughly washed, dried, and stemmed
- ¼ cup olive oil
- 4 to 6 ounces Bulgarian feta cheese
- Salt, for seasoning

• First marinate the onion slices: In a bowl large enough for the finished salad, add the onion slices, stir in the vinegar and mint, and let marinate while you prepare the rest of the salad.

• Cut the watermelon slices into triangles, removing the rind. (We like to repurpose the rind into pickles; see page 55.) Cut each watermelon triangle into 2-inch chunks. You'll end up with 2 to 3 cups.

• Slice the olives in half or into rings.

• Add the spinach to the bowl, turning with salad forks or tongs until evenly coated with the marinated onion.

• Dress with the oil, tossing until evenly coated.

• Gradually add the watermelon. (You may not use it all.) Add the feta cheese and black olives, tossing until evenly mixed.

• Taste for acidity and salt, adding more vinegar and salt as needed. Top with any leftover watermelon and sprinkle on some mint leaves.

Making: Spinach Salad with Watermelon, Feta & Olives

"We add the vinegar first to let it soak into the spinach. If you add the oil first, it will coat the leaves and keep the vinegar from seasoning the greens!" —STEVE

"Bulgarian feta makes all the difference!" —MIKE

METHOD

Watermelon Rind Pickles

Makes 2 heaping cups

It's so rewarding to transform something that normally goes in the compost into something delicious. These crunchy little numbers are great for snacking, on a charcuterie board, or as an addition to salads (like this one). For a softer, more jellylike texture, cook the rinds first in boiling salted water for about 10 minutes or until translucent and then proceed with the recipe. Make sure to remove and discard all but the white parts of the rinds; otherwise your pickles will be tough.

- 1 teaspoon salt, plus more for salting the rind
- 2 cups watermelon rind, white parts only, cut into small cubes
- 1 cup water
- ½ cup red wine vinegar
- ½ cup sugar
- 1 tablespoon ground sumac

• Liberally salt the rinds and let sit for about 30 minutes. Rinse and drain.

• Make the brine: Combine the water, vinegar, sugar, sumac, and the 1 teaspoon of salt in a small saucepan. Bring to a boil, stirring until the sugar is dissolved. Remove from the heat and add the rinds.

• Let the rinds cool in the liquid before pouring into a jar. Cover and refrigerate for 24 hours before serving; keeps well for several weeks.

Avocado Salad with Peaches

Makes 4 servings

This salad is an example of how freeing yourself from a slavish devotion to a recipe can minimize stress and maximize flavor in the kitchen. We originally wrote this recipe using persimmons, but we photographed the dish over the summer with nary a persimmon in sight. We think it's pretty delicious with peaches. And nectarines. We'll make it with persimmons, too.

- 1 large ripe peach or nectarine (or 2 Fuyu or Hachiya persimmons), cut into 2-inch pieces
- Salt, for seasoning
- 1 lemon, halved
- 2 large ripe avocados
- 2 teaspoons Schug (see METHOD, page 58), plus 2 tablespoons neutral oil, such as canola
- 2 tablespoons olive oil
- Ricotta salata or pecorino cheese, for topping

• In a small bowl, season the peach pieces with salt and a generous squeeze of lemon juice.

• Slice each avocado in half crosswise. Scoop out the flesh of each half in one piece, then slice widthwise and fan out on a large platter.

• Squeeze lemon juice over the avocados, and season with salt.

• Spoon the seasoned peaches on top of the avocados. Dress with a few spoonfuls of schug, loosened with the neutral oil, and drizzle everything with the olive oil.

• Just before serving, grate the cheese over the top like a snowfall. This salad won't wait; it's best eaten immediately.

"I usually slice avocados lengthwise, but for this salad, widthwise just looks better."—*STEVE*

METHOD

Schug

Makes 1 heaping pint

We can't get enough of this stuff—we put it on everything. If you want to dial down the heat a bit, try replacing some of the jalapeño peppers with milder poblanos.

- 10 jalapeño peppers, stemmed, seeded, and roughly chopped
- 1 bunch cilantro, thick bottom stems removed
- 1 bunch parsley, thick bottom stems removed
- 4 garlic cloves
- 1 tablespoon salt
- 1 tablespoon ground coriander
- 1 tablespoon ground cumin
- 1½ teaspoons ground cardamom
- 1½ teaspoons ground ginger
- Juice of 1 lemon
- ½ cup neutral oil, such as canola

• Place all the ingredients except the oil in the bowl of a food processor. Pulse repeatedly into a coarse paste (stopping to scrape down the sides of the bowl with a spatula). Transfer to a bowl or jar and stir in the oil.

• Keeps in the refrigerator for up to a week. Cover with oil to keep longer.

Tehina Caesar Salad
with Gutsy Croutons

Makes 4 servings

This is a gutsy salad, with romaine wedges, big, chunky croutons loaded with parsley and cheese, and a tehina dressing that kicks old-school caesar to the curb.

- 1 head romaine lettuce, divided
- 4 cups Gutsy Croutons (see METHOD, page 63)
- Tehina Caesar Dressing (recipe at right)
- Grated Parmigiano or Grana Padano cheese, for sprinkling

• Divide the romaine and croutons among four plates. Spoon the tehina dressing over the salad. Sprinkle generously with cheese.

Tehina Caesar Dressing

Makes 3 cups

- 2 garlic cloves
- Juice of 2 lemons, plus more to taste
- 2 teaspoons anchovy paste (or 2 anchovy fillets, rinsed)
- 4 teaspoons Worcestershire sauce
- ½ teaspoon ground black pepper
- 1½ teaspoons salt, plus more to taste
- 11 ounces tehina paste, stirred with a fork to work through the chunks
- 1 to 1¼ cups cold water

• Pulverize the garlic in a food processor. Add the lemon juice and anchovy paste, pulsing until well-blended. Add the Worcestershire, black pepper, and salt, pulsing a few times. Add the tehina, pulsing until blended.

• While the motor is running, gradually add the water until the mixture is smooth, creamy, and pourable. Taste for acidity and salt, adding more lemon juice or salt as needed.

• Cover and refrigerate extra dressing.

"Caesar salad is universal.
Tehina punches it up even more."—MIKE

"Parsley and bread, olive oil and Parm
equal umami! It's excessive. But great!"—STEVE

METHOD

Gutsy Croutons

Makes 6 cups

The amount of olive oil and cheese in these croutons may seem like a lot, but it does explain why you will not be able to stop eating them.

- 1 day-old baguette
- ½ bunch parsley, stemmed and finely chopped
- 1 cup olive oil
- 1 cup grated Parmigiano-Reggiano or Grana Padano cheese
- Salt and ground black pepper, for seasoning

• Slice the bread in half, then slice each half lengthwise. Cut each piece into 2-inch cubes.

• In a large bowl, stir together the bread cubes, parsley, olive oil, and cheese. Season well with salt and black pepper. Toss the cubes with your hands until evenly coated. Let sit for an hour so the bread cubes are nice and juicy.

• When ready to bake, preheat the oven to 325°F.

• Transfer the cubes into a casserole or baking dish.

• Bake for 20 minutes, then turn the cubes and cook for another 10 to 15 minutes, until golden.

• Leftover croutons store well in an airtight container for a few days.

Kale Salad with Pomegranates

Makes 4 servings

Blitzing the kale in a food processor is a time-saver that transforms the dark leafy green from dry and tough to tender and juicy. When pomegranates are in season, we eat them to excess. Too often, pomegranates are a mere gesture in a dish—a few lonely seeds scattered on top. This salad calls for more than enough to consider reserving a few spoonfuls as a treat for the chef. There's nothing more luxurious than a giant spoonful of pomegranate seeds (except, perhaps, caviar).

> "Seek out Sicilian pistachios if you can—they're worth the splurge!" —*MIKE*

- ½ medium red onion, sliced into half-moons
- Scant ½ cup red wine vinegar
- 1 tablespoon salt
- 2 pomegranates
- 2 bunches kale, ribs removed
- 1 cup unsalted pistachios, roughly chopped
- ⅓ cup olive oil, plus more as needed
- 2 to 4 mandarin oranges (depending on size), peeled and separated into segments

• In a bowl large enough for the entire salad, stir together the red onion, vinegar, and salt.

• Prep the pomegranates: Have a bowl handy for the seeds. Slice each pomegranate in half horizontally. Working with one half at a time, whack the skin side with a wooden spoon to loosen the seeds directly into the bowl. Remove the pith and discard.

• Blitz the kale in a food processor until it looks like finely chopped parsley. Add to the bowl with the marinated onion, stirring until evenly coated. Let sit for 10 minutes to allow the kale to absorb the dressing.

• Add three-quarters of the pistachios plus the olive oil, tossing until evenly coated. Scatter three-quarters of the pomegranate seeds and oranges on top, then stir everything together. Scatter the remaining nuts and fruit on top.

• Drizzle more olive oil on top if you like.

Making: Kale Salad with Pomegranates

"I'm pissing off every European chef by Robot-Coupe-ing kale! But look at the texture! It's tabouli!" —*MIKE*

“Halve the pomegranate over a big bowl, whack the back of each half with a big wooden spoon, and the seeds just pop out.” —*STEVE*

Instructions often call for harvesting pomegranate seeds over a bowl of water so that the pith can rise to the top and be skimmed away. But this sacrifices all of the beautiful juices that make a ripe pomegranate especially luscious. Collect the seeds in an empty bowl and pick out the pith by hand. It’s therapeutic. Plus, a little pith never hurt anyone.

Carrot & Raisin Salad
with Red Cabbage

Makes 8 servings

This carrot and raisin salad was a staple of our dinner table when we were growing up—a classic American recipe that dates to at least *The Fannie Farmer Cookbook*. It was a favorite for those of us who could get past the mayonnaise. Moroccan Jews brought carrot salads with them to Israel in the 1940s, where they are often referred to as gezer chai, or "living carrots" (whatever that means). This version borrows from both traditions and is bright and fresh thanks to a generous amount of herbs and a light dressing. The box grater does a better job than the food processor at giving the carrots a silky texture, plus it's much easier to clean!

- ½ cup golden raisins
- ¼ cup apple cider vinegar
- 1 teaspoon sugar
- 4 large carrots
- ½ to 1 teaspoon salt
- ¼ large red cabbage (about 5 cups cut)
- 2 heaping tablespoons Dijon mustard
- 4 scallions
- 1 bunch cilantro, stemmed and finely chopped
- ½ cup stemmed and finely chopped dill

• In a bowl large enough to hold the entire salad, stir together the raisins, vinegar, and sugar.

• Using a box grater, grate the carrots directly over the raisins. Stir in ½ teaspoon of the salt.

• Finely chop the cabbage and add to the bowl. Add the mustard, stirring until evenly coated. Taste for salt, adding more as needed.

• Slice the scallions into rings, using both the white and pale green parts. Add to the bowl, followed by the cilantro and dill. Stir and let sit for 30 minutes before serving.

• The salad keeps well in the refrigerator for at least 3 days.

"In a half hour, this salad will be perfect. And it'll still be great after a night in the fridge." —*MIKE*

Winter Green Salad
with Schug Dressing

Makes 4 servings

We love making this pale green monochromatic salad as a harbinger of spring and to help brighten our mood during the depths of winter. This salad is best eaten the day it's made.

- Juice of 2 lemons
- ¼ cup olive oil
- 1 to 2 tablespoons Schug (see METHOD, page 58)
- 1 to 1½ teaspoons salt
- 1 fennel bulb, fronds reserved and core removed
- 4 small celery ribs (plus leaves, if you have them), thinly sliced
- 1 tart green apple, such as Granny Smith, thinly sliced
- 20 seedless green grapes, halved
- 2 Persian cucumbers, thinly sliced on the diagonal
- 4 scallions, white and light green parts thinly sliced into rings
- ½ cup stemmed and finely chopped parsley
- ¼ cup fresh mint leaves

• Make the dressing: In a bowl large enough for the entire salad, stir together the lemon juice, olive oil, schug, and salt.

• Thinly slice the fennel and add to the dressing. Toss until evenly coated. Finely chop the fennel fronds and add to the bowl.

• Add the celery, apple, grapes, cucumbers, scallions, and parsley, stirring until evenly coated.

• Tear the mint leaves and scatter on top.

“This is a Big Personality Salad. We can eat off salads like these for a week. Two forks, one bowl.” —*MIKE*

Green Vegetable Salad
with Roasted Tomato–Amba Dressing

Makes 4 servings

Think of this recipe as a guideline for cleaning out the vegetable bin in your fridge. Prep the veggies while making the dressing, which takes about 30 minutes but is totally worth it.

- 1 small head broccoli, stems and florets separated (2 to 3 cups)
- ½ pound snap beans, cut into 1-inch pieces
- ¼ cup water
- Salt, for seasoning
- 1 cup frozen peas, thawed (or a large handful of fresh snow peas or sugar snap peas, trimmed)
- 1 green bell pepper, roughly chopped
- 2 Persian cucumbers, cut into ½-inch pieces
- ½ cup stemmed and finely chopped parsley
- ¼ cup stemmed and finely chopped dill
- 1 bunch chives, cut into ringlets
- 1 cup Roasted Tomato–Amba Dressing (see METHOD, page 74)

• Place the broccoli and beans in a microwave-friendly bowl, along with the water and a sprinkling of salt. Steam until crisp-tender, about 2 minutes.

• Let cool. Drain and transfer to a bowl large enough for the entire salad. Add the rest of the vegetables and herbs, resisting the urge to stir.

• Pour the cooled dressing on top—now you can stir!

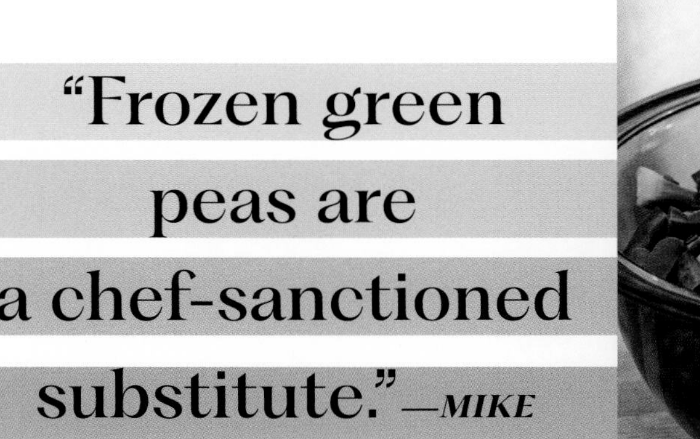

METHOD

Roasted Tomato—Amba Dressing

Makes 1 cup

A touch of amba, the Iraqi pickled mango condiment, amps up the umami of the tomatoes, and the fenugreek in the amba acts as an emulsifier. This sauce could really be eaten all on its own, and it's perfection as an accompaniment to simply cooked fish.

- 1 pint cherry tomatoes
- 2 large garlic cloves, halved
- 6 tablespoons olive oil
- 1 teaspoon salt
- ¼ teaspoon ground black pepper
- 1 tablespoon amba
- 1 tablespoon red wine vinegar

• Preheat the oven to 425°F.

• Place the tomatoes, garlic, and 4 tablespoons of the olive oil in a baking dish or ovenproof skillet. Stir until the tomatoes are evenly coated with the oil. Season with ½ teaspoon of the salt and the black pepper.

• Roast until the tomatoes are bursting, about 30 minutes. Cool to room temperature.

• Transfer the cooled mixture to a medium bowl. Add the amba, breaking up the tomatoes with a whisk.

• Stir in the vinegar, the remaining 2 tablespoons of oil, and the remaining ½ teaspoon of salt. The dressing will be chunky and beguiling.

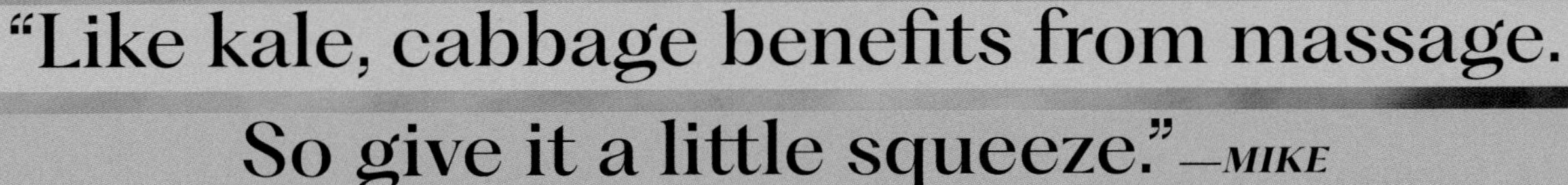
"Like kale, cabbage benefits from massage.
So give it a little squeeze."—MIKE

Green Cabbage
with Caraway, Honey & Chickpeas

Makes 4 generous servings

This is kind of genius. You buy a head of cabbage for almost nothing, add a handful of pantry ingredients, and you've got a salad that can live in your refrigerator for a week! Green cabbage is sweet, cheap, and always in season, but any cabbage would work fine. This reminds us of the lightly fermented cabbage salad at every falafel stand in Israel. Don't skimp on the sumac, the dried sour berry that long predated lemons in the Middle East. We use it like finishing salt here.

- ½ cup white vinegar
- 6 tablespoons olive oil
- 2 tablespoons honey
- 1 tablespoon caraway seeds
- 2 teaspoons salt
- ½ medium onion, thinly sliced into half-moons
- ½ medium green cabbage, finely chopped
- ½ bunch cilantro, finely chopped
- 1 15-ounce can chickpeas, drained
- 1 tablespoon ground sumac

• In a bowl large enough for the entire salad, stir together the vinegar, olive oil, honey, caraway seeds, salt, and onion until the onion is well-coated with all the goodies. Add the cabbage, massaging with your hands until thoroughly coated. The cabbage will shrink in volume.

• Add the cilantro and chickpeas, stirring until evenly mixed.

• Just before serving, sprinkle the sumac on top.

Tunisian Salad

Makes 4 servings

The French influence in North Africa is evident in this Niçoise-like salad that stakes out its own unique identity with the addition of preserved lemon and a gutsy harissa vinaigrette. This is a composed salad, meaning the ingredients are layered on a platter instead of being tossed together. Use a good canned tuna confit; we like it better than ordinary canned tuna and even fresh tuna.

- 1 cup Harissa Dressing (see METHOD, page 81)
- 2 to 3 heads Little Gem or romaine lettuce, leaves separated
- Salt, for seasoning
- 16 ounces canned tuna packed in oil
- 4 hard-cooked eggs, peeled and halved
- 2 to 4 ounces oil-cured Moroccan olives
- 4 to 6 small Yukon potatoes, boiled whole, cooled, and halved
- 3 slices preserved lemon

• Make the dressing in a large bowl, then add the lettuce leaves to the same bowl, keeping any lingering dressing. Sprinkle with salt and toss well.

• Arrange the dressed lettuce on one end of a platter, then the tuna, continuing with the eggs, olives, and potatoes. Top the tuna with the sliced preserved lemons. Serve the lingering dressing on the side.

Making: Tunisian Salad

Beautifully arranged on a platter, this composed salad makes an elegant centerpiece to any lunch. But it's just as good eaten with your hands.

Harissa Dressing

Makes about 1 cup

This recipe may have you asking yourself why more salad dressings aren't spicy.

- Juice of 2 lemons
- 1 to 2 tablespoons harissa, depending on heat preference
- 1 tablespoon honey
- ½ teaspoon salt
- ½ cup olive oil

• In a large bowl, whisk together the lemon juice, harissa, honey, and salt. While whisking, gradually add the olive oil to emulsify the dressing.

2

"Making soup can't be rushed.
Slow down.
Give it the time it needs!" —*MIKE*

Matzo Ball Soup

Makes 16 to 20 matzo balls and 3 quarts soup

Okay. Now the truth can be revealed. In our first book, *Zahav: A World of Israeli Cooking,* 2015, we left out the salt from our matzo ball recipe! We shudder to think how many saltless Friday nights resulted from this error, but we hereby make amends: This recipe calls for 1½ teaspoons salt. We've discovered that cooked matzo balls freeze and reheat really well.

- 4 eggs
- ¼ cup broth, water, or seltzer
- ¼ cup schmaltz, from Instant Pot Chicken Stock (see METHOD, page 88), melted, or neutral oil, such as canola
- 1 cup matzo meal
- 1½ teaspoons salt, plus 1 tablespoon for the water
- ½ teaspoon ground black pepper
- ½ teaspoon baking powder
- 3 quarts Instant Pot Chicken Stock (see METHOD, page 88) or other good chicken stock, hot
- Finely chopped dill sprigs, for finishing

• Whisk together the eggs and liquid in a medium bowl. Whisk in the melted schmaltz.

• With a fork, stir in the matzo meal, salt, black pepper, and baking powder. The mixture may seem overly wet; don't fret.

• Cover with plastic wrap and chill for 30 minutes or longer.

• To a large stockpot filled with at least 6 cups water, add the 1 tablespoon salt. Set over high heat and bring to a boil.

• Have a bowl of cold water ready to moisten your fingers with in between shaping the matzo balls.

• Shape the batter into balls about the size of a golf ball.

• When the water is boiling, drop the matzo balls into the pot, one at a time. They will rise to the surface.

• Cover and cook at a gentle boil (not a rolling boil) for 30 minutes.

• Meanwhile, make sure your chicken stock is good and hot; keep covered until serving.

• Ladle stock into bowls. With a slotted spoon, add two matzo balls to each bowl.

• Finish with dill.

• Refrigerate cooked soup and matzo balls separately. To freeze cooked matzo balls, arrange them on a sheet pan in a single layer. Freeze until solid and then transfer to a freezer bag or container to store. When ready to use, thaw in the refrigerator first. Gently reheat in the chicken stock.

"Set up the batter in the refrigerator for at least thirty minutes. It hydrates the matzo balls." —*STEVE*

Making: Matzo Ball Soup

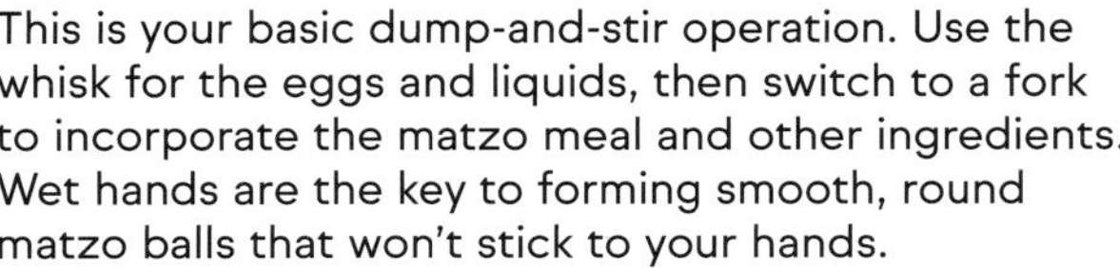

This is your basic dump-and-stir operation. Use the whisk for the eggs and liquids, then switch to a fork to incorporate the matzo meal and other ingredients. Wet hands are the key to forming smooth, round matzo balls that won't stick to your hands.

"In the existential matzo ball debate, we vote for 'floaters' over 'sinkers.' And the real truth: Whenever you try the fancy stuff, it always fails!" —*MIKE*

METHOD

Instant Pot Chicken Stock

Makes about 3 quarts

We prefer kosher chicken for stock or soup—it's pre-salted and makes a very chicken-y broth. The Instant Pot is not the only way to make really good chicken stock, but we like how quickly and easily this recipe comes together on a Friday afternoon. Make your matzo ball mix, throw a chicken in the Instant Pot, and in an hour you can have Shabbat dinner on the table.

Pull apart the cooked chicken meat and add it back into the broth or save it for Tehina Chicken Salad (page 148). To make chicken stock on the stovetop, put the chicken in a large pot, cover well with water, bring it to a boil, skim, and then simmer for two hours. There's nothing wrong with throwing in an onion and some carrots and celery; but sometimes we just like the pure chicken flavors to shine through.

1 small kosher chicken, 2 to 3 pounds
Enough water to cover the chicken, about 3 quarts
1 tablespoon salt

- Place the chicken, water, and salt in your multicooker.
- Program your multicooker to the pressure cooker setting according to the manufacturer's instructions. Make sure the steam release handle is sealed. Set the timer for 50 minutes.
- Completely cool the stock before refrigerating or freezing. The next day, skim the schmaltz off the top and save for matzo balls.

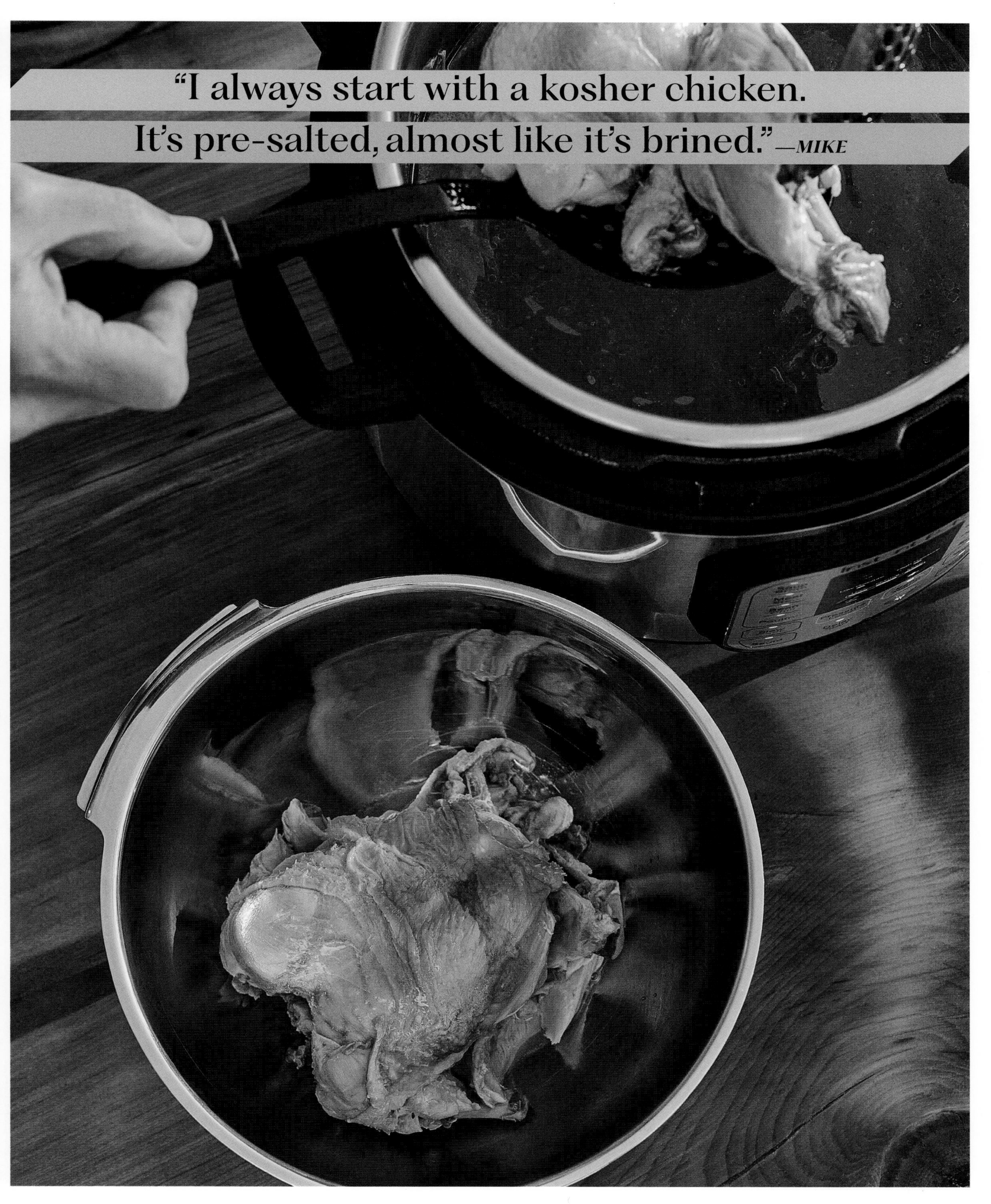
"I always start with a kosher chicken.
It's pre-salted, almost like it's brined."—MIKE

Hot Borscht

Makes about 3 quarts

This cold-weather soup really tugs at our Eastern European DNA. It's worth the effort to make the beef broth, but it's fine to use chicken or vegetable stock instead. There's something about the mingling of the broth with the root vegetables, cabbage, and tomato that makes this soup extra soul-warming. Grating some of the garlic into the hot soup just before serving is an unexpected technique that really wakes up this dish (along with any nearby vampires).

"The sauté step—cooking down the veg in the pot—it's the key to flavor." —*STEVE*

- 6 small or 3 large beets with greens attached (No greens? Use more red cabbage)
- ¼ cup beef fat skimmed from broth, or schmaltz, or even vegetable oil
- ¼ red cabbage, finely chopped (about 2 cups)
- 1 medium carrot, diced
- 1 medium onion, finely chopped
- 4 garlic cloves, chopped fine, plus 1 clove for grating
- 1 tablespoon salt
- ½ teaspoon ground black pepper
- 1 tablespoon tomato paste
- ¼ cup red wine vinegar
- 2 quarts Instant Pot Beef Broth (see METHOD, page 96) or good chicken or vegetable stock
- Cooked meat from Instant Pot Beef Broth (see METHOD, page 96), optional

• Peel and dice the beets, keeping in mind that beets stain . . . everything!

• If using beet greens, wash and rehydrate in a bowl of cold water. Cut away the leaves from the stems, discard the stems, and cut the greens into slivers.

• Melt the beef fat in a large pot. Stir in the cabbage, carrot, onion, and garlic. Cook over medium-low heat until softened, 10 to 12 minutes. Season with the salt and black pepper.

• Add the tomato paste and stir, then add the beets, stirring until coated. Deglaze the vegetables in the pot with the vinegar, stirring and cooking a few minutes until the mixture is dry.

• Stir in the beet greens until evenly coated, then add the broth.

• Cover and bring to a boil. Cook until the vegetables are tender. Just before serving, add the cooked meat if you like, grate the garlic into the pot, and warm through.

Making: Hot Borscht

A lesson in the importance of mise en place: With all your knifework done in advance, this soup comes together quickly and with minimal effort. And please do don an apron and keep paper towels at the ready; beets have no mercy when it comes to staining your clothes and work surfaces.

"We hand-chop the beets 'cause we don't want to get out the food processor. But feel free to use one." —*STEVE*

METHOD

Instant Pot Beef Broth

Makes 3 to 4 quarts

Chicken stock gets all the headlines, but there's still a place in this world for rich and unassuming beef broth. Here again, the Instant Pot makes quick work of a long process, but a large pot and some good bones work well, too. The fat that solidifies on top of the cooled stock can be used to sauté the vegetables for the borscht. And don't forget to scoop the marrow onto a piece of good toast with a sprinkle of salt—the ultimate chef's snack!

- 3 pounds bone-in beef (oxtail, chuck, shanks, or short ribs are all good choices)
- 3 to 4 quarts water, depending on the size of the multicooker
- 1 tablespoon salt
- ½ onion
- 6 garlic cloves, skin on
- 1 large carrot, cut into thirds
- 2 celery ribs, broken

• Place all the ingredients in your multicooker. Program your multicooker to the pressure cooker setting according to the manufacturer's instructions. Make sure the steam release handle is sealed. Set the timer for 50 minutes.

• Cool completely. Remove the meat, chop it finely, and reserve it in the refrigerator for the borscht. Strain the broth and discard the vegetables. Refrigerate overnight. The next day, skim the fat from the broth and reserve for the borscht and other soups.

"I have a confession: I really don't know how to use the Instant Pot!" —*MIKE*

"It's okay. I'll walk you through it." —*STEVE*

Pumpkin Puree
with Dashi & Hawaij

Makes about 2 quarts

Yemenite soup flavored with curry-like hawaij is one of our culinary North Stars for navigating Israeli cuisine, and this East—meets—Farther East mash-up is a versatile recipe—great with other root vegetables (think rutabaga, carrots, or potatoes) or even cauliflower.

¼ cup neutral oil, such as canola
1 large onion, thinly sliced
2 teaspoons salt
4 heaping cups peeled, seeded, and thinly sliced butternut squash
1 scant tablespoon hawaij
5 to 6 cups Dashi (see METHOD, page 100)
1 teaspoon apple cider vinegar
Chopped chives, for finishing

• In a large pot, stir the oil and onion together, turning until evenly coated. Over medium heat, cook until very soft, about 12 minutes.

• While the onions cook down, add the salt; this helps to slow down the browning.

• Add the squash, turning until evenly coated. Cover and reduce the heat to medium-low. Cook the squash until soft, stirring periodically to prevent burning. Break up the squash with the back of a spoon to speed cooking. This should take 15 to 20 minutes.

• Stir in the hawaij and add enough dashi to cover the vegetables. Bring to a simmer. Off heat, puree (we like to use an immersion blender) until smooth; the texture should resemble heavy cream.

• Season with the apple cider vinegar. Sprinkle chives on top of each bowl.

METHOD

Dashi

Makes about 2½ quarts

Dashi is a major building block in Japanese cuisine. It's also the best bang for your buck in terms of stock-making time and effort. The components are water and two pantry ingredients—kombu (dried kelp) and bonito flakes (shavings from a dried and smoked fish in the tuna family). Dashi is ready to go in under twenty minutes and adds a backbone of umami and a subtle smokiness to everything it touches. Whisk in some miso paste, scallions, and cubes of soft tofu and you've got yourself a bowl of miso soup.

- 8 cups water
- 1 6-by-6-inch piece of kombu
- 2 cups bonito flakes (from 2 ounces dry)

• In a large pot, bring the water and kombu just to a boil. Remove it from the heat.

• Add the bonito flakes and let them sink to the bottom. Steep for 5 minutes to let the flavor of the kombu and bonito flakes develop. Then strain and refrigerate.

Making: Pumpkin Puree with Dashi & Hawaij

> "If the veg are not completely cooked in the oil before adding liquid, the soup will be grainy. So we cut the squash into small pieces." —*STEVE*

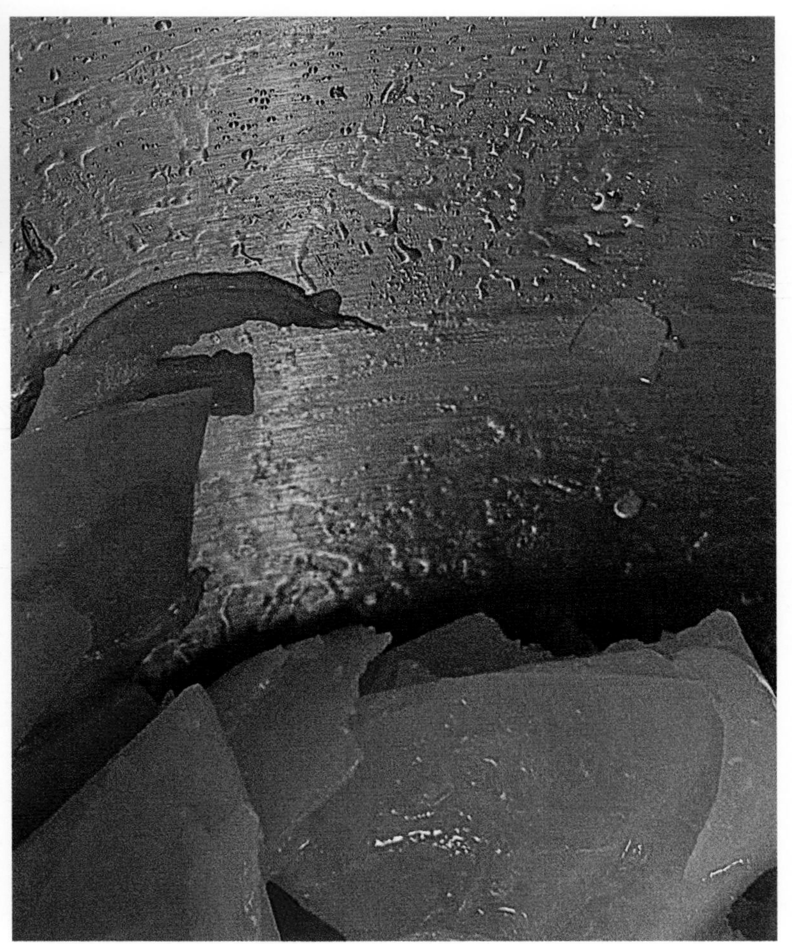

IN PRAISE OF THE IMMERSION BLENDER

We like to use a handheld immersion blender to blend soups right in their cooking pots. It's safer and less messy than transferring the hot soup to a blender container. When pureeing the soup, tilt one edge of the immersion blender ever so slightly away from the bottom of the pot. This will create a vortex that will draw the soup into the blades so it blends evenly and efficiently. But be careful—too much of an angle will cause a splattering mess.

Puree for longer than you think is necessary (or for as long as you can stand the blender noise) for the smoothest texture.

P'Kaila

Makes about 2½ quarts

Fried spinach may sound strange, but it's at the heart of this classic Tunisian-Jewish dish of greens and beans mentioned in the Talmud more than one thousand years ago. Typically, the dish is prepared ahead of time for Shabbat and is part of the traditional Rosh Hashana meal for Tunisian Jews. P'Kaila is usually made with meat, but we take it out for a delicious vegan spin, and it's even better the next day. We recommend eating P'Kaila as Tunisians do—over couscous.

"Be slow and deliberate in cooking this stew, giving it all the time it needs to develop flavor." —*STEVE*

- ¾ cup olive oil
- 1 pound spinach, washed and stemmed
- 1 large onion, very thinly sliced
- 1 teaspoon ground cumin
- 1 teaspoon ground turmeric
- 1 tablespoon salt
- 2 15-ounce cans white beans and their liquid
- 2 large Yukon potatoes, peeled and quartered
- Lemon wedges, for serving

• Put ¼ cup of the oil and all of the spinach into a large pot set over high heat. Use a wooden spoon to stir frequently as you cook down the greens.

• Add ¼ cup more of the oil so that the spinach starts frying, and keep stirring. Cook longer than you think you should—until the spinach is charred and a slight crust forms on the bottom of the pot. This could take up to 20 minutes. The spinach will darken in color to a green-black.

• Remove the greens from the pot and stir in the onion, which will help deglaze the stuck-on bits of spinach. Continue stirring, scraping the bottom of the pot with your wooden spoon.

• Add the remaining ¼ cup of oil, the cumin, turmeric, and salt, stirring until the onion is evenly coated.

• Add the beans (and their liquid) and the potatoes. Fill each empty bean can with water once and add to the pot, then add 2 additional cups of water. Return the spinach to the pot.

• Stir the vegetables together, scraping the bottom of the pot, where some tasty bits may still be lingering. Cover and cook over medium heat for 25 minutes, until the potatoes are tender.

• Serve with lemon wedges.

Making: P'Kaila

The brown bits that the spinach leaves behind on the bottom of the pot (the French call it "fond") have a ton of flavor. So roll up your sleeves and use a wooden spatula to scrape off the fond and dissolve it back into the cooking liquid.

"Who knew that the secret to getting so much flavor out of spinach was to burn it?" —*STEVE*

Harira

Makes about 2½ quarts

Harira is a classic North African soup that is often the first thing Muslims eat to break their Ramadan fast. Likewise, Jews of the region eat harira at the end of Yom Kippur. Harira is typically enriched with a bit of lamb or other meat, but there are as many variations as there are Moroccan grandmothers.

We always keep plenty of Three C's Spice Blend (two parts cumin, two parts coriander, one part caraway, and a pinch of cardamom) on hand for that trademark North African flavor profile. Toasting the noodles brings even more flavor; they cook quickly but soak up liquid, so add them just before serving.

HARIRA PASTE

- 1 cinnamon stick
- 2½ teaspoons Three C's Spice Blend (stir together 1 teaspoon each ground coriander and ground cumin, ½ teaspoon ground caraway, and a pinch or two ground cardamom)
- 3 garlic cloves
- 1 tablespoon peeled and diced fresh ginger
- 2 tablespoons harissa

• With a mortar and pestle or an electric spice grinder, grind the cinnamon stick and the Three C's Spice Blend until powdery.

• If using the mortar, keep going and add the garlic and ginger, or use the small bowl of a food processor to pulverize them into a paste, then add the garlic and ginger.

• Add the harissa and blend evenly.

SOUP

- ½ cup vermicelli, broken into small pieces, or fideo noodles (about 2.2 ounces)
- ¼ cup olive oil
- 2 celery ribs, diced
- 1 large onion, diced
- 1 large carrot, diced
- 2 tablespoons tomato paste
- 1 15-ounce can chickpeas and their liquid
- 1 cup green lentils
- 2 teaspoons salt, plus more as needed
- 5 cups water

• Preheat the oven to 375°F. Toast the vermicelli on a sheet pan, about 5 minutes.

• In a large pot set over medium heat, add the olive oil, celery, onion, and carrot, cooking until softened, 12 to 15 minutes. Stir in the harira paste and tomato paste.

• Add the chickpeas (and their liquid), lentils, salt, and 4 cups of the water. Bring the soup to a boil over high heat. Reduce the heat to medium-low and cover. Cook until the lentils are nearly done, about 25 minutes.

• Add the remaining 1 cup of water, then stir in the toasted vermicelli and cook until tender, 5 to 6 minutes. Serve hot.

Making: Harira

"They taught us in culinary school to have a bowl for each ingredient. Then you're ready for *anything!*" —STEVE

We find it therapeutic to use a mortar and pestle to bash away at the ingredients that form the backbone of our Harira (not to mention the incomparable flavor and aroma of freshly ground spices and aromatics). A spice grinder and food processor are worthy stand-ins for your misdirected aggression.

Note how the noodles are briefly toasted before being added to the soup at the last minute.

Mushroom Freekah Soup

Makes about 2 quarts

This is our turn on the classic mushroom barley soup, using freekah, the smoky green wheat from the Levant, in place of the barley. Rehydrated dried mushrooms and their liquid boost the flavor of the fresh mushrooms. But the real secret ingredient is soy sauce. Your family will never guess what makes this comforting vegan soup so rich and tasty.

- 3 cups boiling water
- ½ cup dried mushrooms, such as shiitakes or porcini
- ⅓ cup soy sauce
- ¼ cup olive oil
- 1 pound cremini mushrooms, quartered, stems trimmed and chopped
- 2 celery ribs, diced
- 2 small carrots, diced
- 1 medium onion, diced
- 4 garlic cloves, minced
- 1 teaspoon salt
- 2 tablespoons tomato paste
- 1 cup freekah
- 1 cup finely chopped chives
- 1 cup finely chopped parsley leaves
- Lemon wedges, for serving

• In a medium bowl, pour the boiling water over the dried mushrooms and soy sauce. Cover and soak until the mushrooms are plump and rehydrated, about 20 minutes.

• In a large heavy-bottomed pot set over high heat, warm the olive oil. Then add the quartered cremini mushroom tops and cook until nice and brown.

• To the soup pot, add the celery, carrots, onion, garlic, and mushroom stems, stirring until evenly coated. Reduce the heat to medium-low and cook until the vegetables are softened, about 10 minutes. You'll develop some nice brown bits on the bottom of the pot.

• Stir the salt and tomato paste into the browning vegetables; cook for a minute.

• Strain out the rehydrated dried mushrooms and finely chop, reserving the soaking liquid. Add both the liquid and the chopped mushrooms to the pot along with 3 cups of water.

• Turn up the heat, cover, and bring to a boil. Then stir the freekah into the soup.

• Cover and reduce the heat to medium-low and cook, stirring occasionally, until the freekah is tender, about 20 minutes.

• Blend briefly with an immersion blender (10 to 15 seconds) to add body to the soup.

• Stir in the chives and parsley. Serve hot, with lemon wedges.

"Don't crowd the pan when cooking mushrooms—we want to brown them, not steam them!"—*MIKE*

Making: Mushroom Freekah Soup

Rehydrate the dried mushrooms in boiling water while you're chopping the vegetables. Fresh mushrooms have a high moisture content, so the trick to browning them is to cook them in a single layer over high heat, without moving them around too much.

"Zhuzh the freekah
in the pot
with a hand blender
just enough
to give a little body
to the soup." —*MIKE*

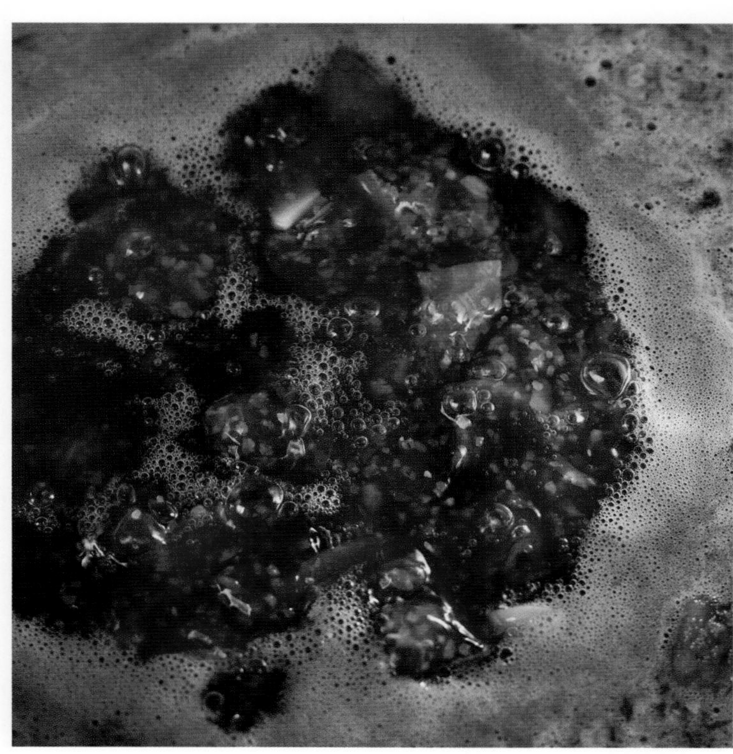

3.

"Spatchcocking is not rocket science; whatever bones you leave in will add to the flavor." —*MIKE*

Chicken

Spatchcock Chicken

Moroccan Seasoning

Hungarian Seasoning
Yemenite Seasoning

To Spatchcock a Chicken

"Spatchcocking" is a fun word that refers to removing the backbone of a chicken and then flattening the carcass. A spatchcocked bird cooks more quickly and evenly than a whole one, and it's a breeze to carve once cooked. Freeze the backbone and make chicken stock (see page 88) as soon as you have accumulated a critical mass.

- We use good-quality kitchen shears for the most control (but a chef's knife works, too).
- Place the chicken on a work surface breast side down, with the neck end closest to you. Cut along the length of spine, one side at a time, and remove the backbone to freeze for chicken stock.
- Keep the chicken splayed open. Place the blade of a chef's knife on top of the keel bone (in the center) and give it a good whack to help flatten the bird. Trim fat as needed.
- Season each side with 1 teaspoon salt.

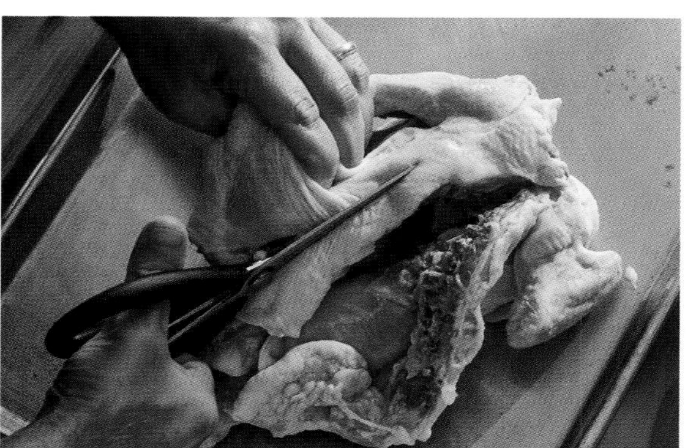

- Generously rub spices on both sides of the chicken (about 1 tablespoon per side). Place skin side up on a sheet pan.
- Preheat the oven to 450°F.
- Arrange accompanying vegetables and aromatics around the flattened chicken. Roast until the juices run clear, about 40 minutes.

Spatchcock Chicken Moroccan Seasoning

Makes 4 servings

Sheet pan dinners are trending for good reason: The oven does all the work, and cleanup is minimal. And a spatchcocked chicken makes a great centerpiece, flavoring its accompaniments with chicken-y goodness. Our Moroccan-themed version features ras el hanout, which is Arabic for "head of the shop," aka "the good stuff." It's a common North African spice blend—sweet and savory—of more than a dozen ingredients. Our quick sweet-and-spicy sauce combines pan juices with harissa and honey.

> "I don't ever peel my carrots, I just wash them." —*MIKE*

- 1 4- to 5-pound chicken, backbone removed and flattened
- 2¼ teaspoons salt
- 2 tablespoons ras el hanout
- 4 large carrots, cut on the diagonal into long pieces
- 2 medium fennel bulbs, root and stalks removed, cut into wedges
- 1 green bell pepper, quartered
- 1 head garlic, skin on, cut in half through the root
- Olive oil, for moistening the vegetables
- 1 tablespoon honey
- 1 tablespoon harissa

• Season each side of the chicken with 1 teaspoon of the salt (a total of 2 teaspoons). Generously rub the ras el hanout on both sides of the chicken (estimating 1 tablespoon per side).

• Place the chicken skin side up on a large sheet pan.

• Preheat the oven to 450°F.

• In a medium bowl, stir together the carrots, fennel, pepper, garlic, and the remaining ¼ teaspoon of salt.

• Add enough oil to lightly coat the vegetables.

• Scatter the vegetables around the chicken. Roast until the chicken juices run clear, 40 to 45 minutes.

• While the chicken rests, pour the pan juices into a small bowl. Stir in the honey and harissa until evenly mixed. Serve at the table as a sauce.

Z

"People are squeamish about how much salt to use. But salt is key: It helps cure and flavor the chicken."—*MIKE*

Spatchcock Chicken Hungarian Seasoning

Makes 4 servings

Nothing says Shabbat dinner like a chicken with a generous rub of paprika, especially if it's a kosher chicken. The potatoes essentially confit in the red-stained schmaltz, adding gravitas to a meal that could see you through a Budapest winter. The pan juices are thickened with the smashed cloves of roasted garlic and brightened with lemon and parsley for passing around the Shabbat table.

- 1 4- to 5-pound chicken, backbone removed and flattened
- 2½ teaspoons salt
- 2 tablespoons paprika
- 1 pound (6 to 8) small potatoes (such as fingerling or Yukon), halved
- ½ large onion, cut into wedges
- 2 red bell peppers, quartered
- 1 head garlic, skin on, cut in half through the root
- Olive oil, for moistening the vegetables
- ¼ cup finely chopped parsley
- Juice of ½ lemon

• Season each side of the chicken with 1 teaspoon of the salt (a total of 2 teaspoons). Generously rub the paprika on both sides of the chicken (estimating 1 tablespoon per side).

• Place the chicken skin side up on a large sheet pan.

• Preheat the oven to 450°F.

• In a medium bowl, stir together the potatoes, onion, peppers, garlic, and ¼ teaspoon of the salt. Add enough oil to lightly coat the vegetables.

• Scatter the vegetables around the chicken. Roast until the chicken juices run clear, 40 to 45 minutes.

• While the chicken rests, make a sauce with the pan juices. Pour the juices into a small bowl. Stir in the parsley, lemon juice, and remaining ¼ teaspoon of salt. Squeeze the roasted garlic into the bowl and mash with a fork.

• Serve the chicken with the sauce on the side.

Spatchcock Chicken Yemenite Seasoning

Makes 4 servings

We love Yemenite chicken soup so much, it only makes sense to apply the same flavors to a spatchcocked chicken dinner. Hawaij, chicken, and potatoes are a time-tested partnership. For the ultimate midnight snack, sandwich leftover chicken between two slices of challah slathered with Schug Tehina.

- 1 4- to 5-pound whole chicken, backbone removed and flattened
- 2¼ teaspoons salt
- 2 tablespoons hawaij
- 4 celery ribs, cut into halves or thirds
- ½ large onion, cut into wedges
- 1 pound (6 to 8) small potatoes (such as fingerling or Yukon), halved
- 1 head garlic, skin on, cut in half through the root
- Olive oil, for moistening the vegetables
- Schug Tehina, for serving (see below at right)

- Season each side of the chicken with 1 teaspoon of the salt (a total of 2 teaspoons). Generously rub the hawaij on both sides of the chicken (estimating 1 tablespoon per side).
- Place the chicken skin side up on a large sheet pan.
- Preheat the oven to 450°F.
- In a medium bowl, stir together the celery, onion, potatoes, garlic, and the remaining ¼ teaspoon of salt.
- Add enough oil to lightly coat the vegetables.
- Scatter the vegetables around the chicken. Roast until the chicken juices run clear, 40 to 45 minutes.
- Serve with Schug Tehina.

Schug Tehina

- In a small bowl, stir together 1 cup Basic Tehina Sauce (page 264) and 1 tablespoon Schug (page 58). Taste and add a squeeze of juice from a lemon half and salt as needed. Keeps well in an airtight container in the refrigerator for up to 1 week.

METHOD

Stovetop Chicken Stock

Makes about 3 quarts

We like the no-waste vibe of repurposing chicken backbones into golden chicken stock on the stovetop. But if the Instant Pot is more your thing, the set-and-forget version is on page 88.

- 3 chicken backbones
- 1 large onion, cut into wedges, plus the skins
- 1 celery rib, cut into thirds
- 1 carrot, cut into thirds or quarters
- 1 garlic head, skin on, cut in half through the root
- 1 handful parsley stems
- Pinch turmeric
- A few pinches salt

• Place all the ingredients in a large pot.

• Add enough water to cover plus an inch, about 12 cups.

• Bring to a boil. Reduce the heat to medium-low, cover, and cook for 2 hours. Cool, strain and discard the solids, and store the stock in the refrigerator or freezer.

Chicken Wings, Three Ways,
with Tehina Ranch Dressing

Makes 4 servings

The secret to restaurant chicken wings? Deep-frying! But the secret to great wings at home is to roast them in a very hot oven, which cooks them through, renders excess fat, and crisps up the skin. Only after roasting do we season the wings. After coating the wings with sauce, we briefly pop them under the broiler to caramelize the glaze. Serve a pile of roasted wings with a bowl of Tehina Ranch Dressing for dunking.

FOR THE WINGS

- 1 tablespoon salt
- 12 whole chicken wings (about 3 pounds), separated into wings and drumettes
- Harissa-Pomegranate Molasses Glaze, Za'atar Rub, or Date Molasses-Urfa Pepper Glaze (page 133), optional
- Tehina Ranch Dressing (recipe follows), for serving

• Preheat the oven to 450°F.

• In a medium bowl, salt the wings well.

• Arrange the wings in a single layer on a sheet pan. (Or, put the wings on a rack inside the sheet pan, which allows the fat to drip off and makes for a crispier skin.) Place on the middle rack in the oven and roast until the skin is golden, 35 to 40 minutes.

• While the wings cook, whip up one or all three of the final sauce flavors. You'll want a separate bowl for each flavor.

Tehina Ranch Dressing

Makes 1½ cups

This nondairy version of ranch dressing is also a fully qualified salad dressing. And it's great with crudités, too!

- 1 cup Basic Tehina Sauce (see METHOD, page 264)
- ½ cup stemmed and finely chopped parsley
- ½ cup stemmed and finely chopped dill
- ½ cup finely chopped chives
- Juice of ½ lemon
- 1½ teaspoons onion powder
- 1½ teaspoons garlic powder
- ½ teaspoon ground black pepper
- ½ teaspoon salt

• Stir together all the ingredients in a medium bowl until evenly mixed.

• The sauce will be thick. Gradually add water to thin it, using a fork to whisk. We like our dressing thick enough to cling to a roasted wing.

"Mike and I like to talk through our recipes. We cook with words first."—*STEVE*

Sheet pan chicken wings just out of the oven and ready to munch on. From the top: Date Molasses—Urfa Pepper Glaze, Harissa-Pomegranate Molasses Glaze, Za'atar Rub.

Chicken Wings, Three Flavors

Makes about ½ cup each

Harissa–Pomegranate Molasses Glaze

We used this glaze on our grilled chicken wings at Laser Wolf. It has every flavor you could ask for: sweet, sour, and spicy.

- ½ cup pomegranate molasses
- 2 tablespoons harissa
- ½ teaspoon salt

• A medium bowl will seem too big, but that's what you'll need to evenly coat the wings. Stir the ingredients together until the mixture is smooth.

• Add the cooked wings to the glaze. Use tongs to turn the wings on all sides until they are thoroughly coated.

Za'atar Rub

Chicken loves za'atar like Joanie loves Chachi. Adding a bit of olive oil to the za'atar in the bowl with the wings helps the sauce adhere.

- 2 tablespoons za'atar
- 1 teaspoon olive oil

• Put the za'atar, then the olive oil into a medium bowl you'll use to toss the wings.

• Then add the cooked wings, using tongs to turn the wings on all sides until they are thoroughly coated.

Date Molasses–Urfa Pepper Glaze

Intense heat does not overpower the flavor of Urfa biber, a sun-dried Turkish pepper. Its raisiny and chocolaty notes pair exceptionally well with date molasses.

- ½ cup date molasses
- 1 tablespoon ground Urfa pepper
- ½ teaspoon salt
- Zest of 1 orange
- Juice of ½ lemon, for serving

• In a medium bowl, stir the molasses, Urfa pepper, salt, and orange zest together until the mixture is smooth.

• Add the cooked wings to the glaze. Use tongs to turn the wings on all sides until they are thoroughly coated.

• Squeeze lemon juice all over the wings just before serving.

Arabic Coffee BBQ Chicken
with Red Cabbage Slaw

Makes 4 servings

This is an easy, no-cook barbecue sauce that can be thrown together in no time using staple pantry ingredients. The cardamom is a nod to Arabic coffee and lends a bit of an exotic edge to the standard cast of American barbecue sauce characters.

- ½ cup brown sugar
- 1½ teaspoons ground cardamom
- 1 teaspoon onion powder
- 1 teaspoon salt
- ½ cup hot brewed coffee
- 1 cup ketchup
- ¼ cup prepared mustard
- 4 teaspoons Worcestershire sauce
- 4 boneless, skinless chicken breasts
- ½ cup Basic Tehina Sauce (see METHOD, page 264)
- 4 soft hamburger buns or potato rolls
- Red Cabbage Slaw (page 136)

• Make the marinade: In a medium bowl, stir together the brown sugar, cardamom, onion powder, and salt. Pour the coffee on top, stirring until the sugar is dissolved. Stir in the ketchup, mustard, and Worcestershire. You'll end up with 2 cups.

• Measure out half of the sauce and coat the chicken. Reserve the remaining sauce.

• Marinate the chicken at room temperature for 1 hour.

• When ready to cook, arrange the chicken in a single layer on a sheet pan. Set the oven to the low broiler setting and broil for 10 minutes.

• Measure out a half cup of the reserved BBQ sauce and brush on top of the chicken. Set the broiler setting to high. Adjust the rack as needed if the sauce begins to burn. Broil until the chicken is cooked through, 10 to 15 minutes.

• When the chicken is cool to the touch, cut crosswise into ¼-inch slices.

• In a small bowl, stir together the remaining ½ cup of the BBQ sauce and the Basic Tehina Sauce.

• Pile chicken on the bottom of each bun. Top with a heaping spoonful of tehina BBQ sauce, then the Red Cabbage Slaw, and press together with the top bun.

“At home, I always add coffee to a sauce—just whatever’s left in the pot.” —*STEVE*

Red Cabbage Slaw

Makes 4 servings, plus lots of leftovers

We love the way a bit of sugar balances out the vinegar in this mayo-less slaw. Prepare it ahead to let the salt and sugar work their magic on the vegetables—their texture becomes almost silky. Our favorite way to prep bell peppers for slicing or chopping starts with cutting off the top and bottom. Then make a perpendicular incision and follow the inside of the pepper with a chef's knife, rotating the pepper as you go, removing the core and seeds along with the white ribs. Now you've "unrolled" the pepper into one long sheet, ready to be sliced or diced.

- ½ medium red cabbage, finely chopped (4 to 5 cups)
- 1 tablespoon salt
- 1 tablespoon sugar
- 1 green bell pepper, julienned
- 1 red bell pepper, julienned
- 2 large carrots, grated
- 2 tablespoons white wine vinegar or apple cider vinegar

• In a large bowl, stir together all the ingredients until evenly mixed.

• Let sit for at least 30 minutes before serving. The slaw is even better the next day.

Mango Chicken & Rice

Makes 4 servings

We're not the biggest fans of the ubiquitous boneless, skinless chicken breasts, but there's a time and a place for them, especially when you're trying to get a weeknight dinner on the table. Marinate the chicken first, and by the time the rice is done, a quick broil is all you need to finish the chicken. Kids especially love this mango rice.

FOR THE RICE

- 2 cups jasmine rice, rinsed
- 3 cups water
- 1 teaspoon salt
- 1 ripe mango, cut into cubes
- 1 bunch scallions, finely chopped
- ½ cup chopped cilantro leaves
- 1 tablespoon neutral oil

• Place the rinsed rice in a medium saucepan and add the water and ½ teaspoon of the salt. Cover and bring to a boil.

• Reduce the heat to low and cook for 20 minutes. Off the heat, keep covered and let the rice rest for 20 minutes.

• Transfer the rice to a medium bowl. Gently fold in the remaining ½ teaspoon of salt, the mango, scallions, cilantro, and oil until evenly mixed.

FOR THE CHICKEN

- ½ large onion, very thinly sliced
- 1 cup mango puree (or canned mango nectar)
- 2 tablespoons neutral oil
- 2½ teaspoons salt
- ¼ teaspoon ground cayenne pepper
- 4 boneless, skinless chicken breasts, cut into 2-inch chunks

• Place all the ingredients in a nonreactive bowl and stir together until the chicken is thoroughly coated.

• Cover and marinate for 1 hour at room temperature or longer in the refrigerator.

• Remove the chicken from the marinade and arrange on a sheet pan in a single layer.

• Set the oven to the high broiler setting. Cook the chicken until the juices run clear, 10 to 12 minutes.

• Serve with the mango rice.

"Instead of in the fridge, I prefer to do marinades at room temp for one to two hours." —*MIKE*

"Use the chicken-poaching liquid to cook freekah or other grains. It's the circle of life!" —*MIKE*

Hawaij Poached Chicken
with Avocado & Green Tehina

Makes 4 servings

Here's our favorite way to cook chicken breasts: Drop them in hot liquid and quickly return to a boil. Turn off the heat and let the chicken gently "steep" until cooked through. Keep the chicken in the poaching liquid until ready to serve, or refrigerate overnight and serve cold. The longer the chicken spends in the broth, the more flavor it will have! And leftover broth can become soup.

FOR THE CHICKEN

- 1 quart Stovetop Chicken Stock (see METHOD, page 129) or any good chicken stock
- 1 teaspoon salt, plus more for seasoning
- 2 tablespoons hawaij
- 4 boneless, skinless chicken breasts
- Green Tehina (recipe follows)
- 1 ripe avocado
- 1 ripe beefsteak tomato, sliced
- 1 serrano or jalapeño pepper, thinly sliced into rings
- ¼ cup stemmed and chopped cilantro

• Choose a pan or pot big enough for the chicken breasts to poach in a single layer.

• Add the chicken stock, salt, and hawaij, whisking until dissolved over medium heat. Cover and bring to a boil.

• Lightly season the chicken with salt on both sides. Carefully drop the chicken breasts, one at a time, into the stock. Return to a boil.

• Cover and turn off the heat. The chicken will passively cook; check for doneness at 25 minutes.

• To assemble the salad, spoon Green Tehina onto a platter or large serving plate.

• Halve, pit, and peel the avocado, then slice.

• Slice the chicken crosswise and layer on top of the Green Tehina.

• Arrange the avocado and tomato on the platter; season with salt. Scatter the chile pepper rings on top, then the cilantro.

Green Tehina

Makes 2 cups

A two-to-one herb—tehina sauce ratio will color the sauce more green than beige.

- 2 cups stemmed and chopped leafy herbs (any combination of parsley, cilantro, chives, dill, and mint)
- 1 cup Basic Tehina Sauce (see METHOD, page 264)
- Salt
- Ice water

• Pulverize the herbs in a food processor with a few tablespoons of the tehina sauce to encourage the chlorophyll to release. Add the rest of the sauce and a pinch of salt.

• Blend until the herbs are chopped into specks, adding ice water to thin as necessary.

Sesame Chicken with Matbucha

Makes 4 servings

When we were growing up, it sometimes felt like we ate chicken every night; our mothers were constantly trying to find new ways to serve it. This recipe is dedicated to parents everywhere—we know what it means to feed a bunch of picky children! It's super simple, but the results are visually stunning (and taste pretty great, too). The secret is matbucha, a tomato–bell pepper sauce.

> "Sesame seeds are the Israeli Shake 'n Bake." —*MIKE*

FOR THE MATBUCHA

- ¼ cup olive oil
- ½ large onion, minced
- 4 large garlic cloves, thinly sliced
- 1 red bell pepper, finely diced
- 2 tablespoons tomato paste
- 1 teaspoon salt
- 1 teaspoon paprika
- 2 large tomatoes, cut into medium dice

• Pour the oil into a large skillet set over medium heat. Add the onion, garlic, and pepper and cook until slightly softened, 5 to 7 minutes.

• Stir in the tomato paste, salt, and paprika until the vegetables are evenly coated. Add the tomatoes, stirring until evenly mixed. Cook until the tomatoes are dissolved, 10 to 15 minutes.

• Let rest off the heat while you prepare the chicken. Gently reheat when ready to serve.

FOR THE CHICKEN

- 4 bone-in, skin-on chicken thighs, or boneless, skinless chicken thighs, or chicken breasts
- Salt, for seasoning
- ¼ cup tehina paste, loosened with a fork
- ½ cup sesame seeds

• Preheat the oven to 350°F.

• Liberally season both sides of the chicken thighs with salt. Brush the skin side with tehina paste.

• Scatter the sesame seeds on a platter or in a shallow dish.

• Press the tehina-coated chicken into the sesame seeds.

• Arrange in a baking dish or on a sheet pan seeds side up. Bake until the chicken is golden brown on top and the juices run clear, 45 to 55 minutes.

• Serve with the warmed matbucha on the side.

Making: Sesame Chicken with Matbucha

Paint the chicken pieces with a thin coating of tehina and then dunk it into a bowl of sesame seeds. Shake the bowl a bit and lightly press down on the chicken to ensure even coverage. Here we hold the chicken by the bone to avoid disturbing the uniform coating of seeds. Use a fork for boneless chicken pieces.

Chicken with Apricots, Almonds & Bulgur

Makes 4 servings

This simple baked chicken dish—elevated with dried apricots and sliced almonds—can easily make the transition from weeknight supper to celebration meal. The chicken is seasoned with spices from North Africa (the Three C's), where cooking meat with dried fruit is a proven winner. The bulgur wheat is easy to prepare and excels at soaking up all the delicious juices.

"This looks like Shabbat dinner." —*MIKE*

- 2 cups medium-grind bulgur
- 2 teaspoons salt, plus more for seasoning
- 4 cups hot chicken stock or water
- 4 bone-in, skin-on chicken thighs
- 2½ teaspoons Three C's Spice Blend (stir together 1 teaspoon each ground coriander and ground cumin, ½ teaspoon ground caraway, and a pinch or two ground cardamom)
- ½ cup tomato puree
- 2 tablespoons red wine vinegar
- 1 cup dried apricots
- 1 cup sliced almonds
- 4 teaspoons honey

• Put the bulgur and 1½ teaspoons of the salt into a medium heat-proof bowl. Ladle 3 cups of the hot liquid on top. Cover with plastic wrap and let sit until the liquid has been absorbed, about 20 minutes.

• Meanwhile, prep the chicken: Liberally season with the Three C's and salt on both sides. Transfer to a baking dish, skin side up.

• Preheat the oven to 375°F.

• In another medium bowl, stir together the tomato puree, red wine vinegar, and the remaining 1 cup of hot liquid. Stir in the remaining ½ teaspoon of salt. Pour on top of the chicken. Add the apricots and half of the almonds.

• Bake until the chicken juices run clear, 45 to 50 minutes.

• Drizzle each thigh with 1 teaspoon of the honey. Return the chicken to the oven to brown on top, about 5 minutes.

• Fluff the bulgur with a fork. Arrange on a platter. Spoon on the chicken, sauce, and apricots, and scatter the remaining almonds on top.

Tehina Chicken Salad

Makes 1½ quarts

Here is a lighter version of chicken salad that will have your guests saying, "I can't believe there's no mayo!" Feel free to use a supermarket rotisserie chicken for this dish.

- 1 roasted chicken (2 to 3 pounds), cool to the touch
- 2 celery ribs, finely chopped
- 1 bunch scallions, thinly sliced into rings
- ½ cup chopped cilantro leaves
- 1 cup Basic Tehina Sauce (see METHOD, page 264)
- Juice of ½ lemon
- 1 teaspoon salt
- ½ teaspoon ground black pepper
- Romaine lettuce leaves or toast, for serving

• Peel the skin from the chicken and pull the meat off the bones. Finely chop the meat, or shred with your hands. Transfer to a large bowl.

• Add all the other ingredients, resisting the urge to stir between additions.

• With a big spoon, now stir until the chicken is evenly coated with all the goodies.

• Serve on romaine leaves or your favorite toast.

"I want to use the whole lettuce leaf. Is that cool with you?" —*MIKE*

"Sure!" —*STEVE*

Green Shakshuka

Red Shakshuka

Red Shakshuka

Makes 4 servings

Shakshuka is a great way to feed a crowd, but getting the eggs right is trickier than it looks. Often, the yolks are perfect while the whites are still undercooked. To solve that problem, we use a nontraditional method: We fry the eggs first to set the whites, and then add the sauce to the pan to heat up while the yolks achieve that magical balance between liquid and solid states.

- 2 red bell peppers, cut into large dice
- 1 large onion, cut into eighths
- 1 head garlic, cloves peeled and separated
- ¾ cup olive oil
- 1 tablespoon salt, plus more for seasoning
- 2 large beefsteak or 4 Roma tomatoes, coarsely chopped
- 2 tablespoons harissa
- 8 eggs
- ½ cup chopped parsley

- Put the peppers, onion, and garlic in a medium bowl. Add ½ cup of the olive oil and the salt, stirring until evenly coated.
- Transfer the vegetables to a sheet pan and arrange in a single layer.
- Set the oven to the low broiler setting. Cook until well-charred, about 30 minutes. Let cool.
- Remove just the onion and finely chop. Transfer to a bowl, along with the rest of the charred vegetables and any residual juices. Lightly mash for a more uniform texture. Add the chopped tomatoes and stir in the harissa.
- Crack the eggs into a medium bowl.
- Set a large skillet over high heat. Pour in the remaining ¼ cup of olive oil. Carefully add the eggs, one at a time, and lightly salt. Reduce the heat to medium and cook until the whites are set.
- Transfer the vegetable mixture to the skillet, being careful not to break the egg yolks. Cook until the sauce is warmed through and the egg yolks are set, 8 to 10 minutes.
- Portion into bowls, sprinkle parsley over the top, and serve.

Green Shakshuka

Makes 4 servings

Shakshuka is a gutsy, spicy dish and we're able to add even more depth of flavor by charring the vegetables under the broiler (this is also a big time saver). Tomatillo-based Green Shakshuka spiced with schug is a fun twist on the traditional tomato-based Red Shakshuka. We recommend serving both at your next Christmas-themed brunch!

"Here's a shakshuka shocker: We broil our vegetables instead of baking them!" —*STEVE*

- 12 tomatillos, husked, rinsed, and quartered
- 2 large green bell peppers, cut into large dice
- 1 large onion, cut into 2-inch wedges
- 1 head garlic, cloves peeled and separated
- ¾ cup olive oil
- 2 teaspoons salt, plus more for seasoning
- 2 tablespoons Schug (see METHOD, page 58)
- 8 eggs
- ½ cup chopped cilantro leaves

• Put the tomatillos, peppers, onion, and garlic in a large bowl. Add ½ cup of the olive oil and the salt, stirring until evenly coated.

• Transfer the vegetables to a sheet pan in a single layer.

• Set the oven to the low broiler setting. Cook until well-charred, about 30 minutes. Let cool.

• Remove just the onion and finely chop. Transfer to a bowl, along with the rest of the charred vegetables and any residual juices. Lightly mash for a more uniform texture, and stir in the schug.

• Crack the eggs into a medium bowl.

• Set a large skillet over high heat. Pour in the remaining ¼ cup of olive oil. Carefully add the eggs, one at a time, and lightly salt. Reduce the heat to medium and cook until the whites are set.

• Transfer the vegetable mixture to the skillet, being careful not to break the egg yolks. Cook until the sauce is warmed through and the egg yolks are set, 8 to 10 minutes.

• Portion into bowls, sprinkle cilantro over the top, and serve.

Making: Green (& Red) Shakshuka

"You've gotta hand-mix the shakshuka ingredients. You can't be afraid to touch the food!" —*MIKE*

"We love half sheet pans so much, we should sell them!" —*MIKE*

Mix the cut vegetables in a bowl with olive oil and salt. Transfer to a sheet pan in a single layer and broil in the oven until well-charred, about 30 minutes. Let cool. Remove the onion, finely chop, and return to the rest of the vegetables in the bowl. Add the eggs to the skillet, one by one. When the eggs are set, carefully transfer in the cooked vegetables. Sprinkle cilantro on top and serve in individual bowls.

Tehina Amba Egg Salad

Makes 4 servings

This idea emerged from a conversation about sabich, our favorite sandwich of Iraqi parentage. Sabich features fried eggplant, hard-cooked egg, and amba. It's one of those odd combinations that just works, and we think it does especially well in this egg salad version. We love the way the egg and tehina temper the assertively funky amba. Just trust us on this one.

- 8 hard-cooked eggs, peeled and quartered
- 1½ teaspoons amba
- ¼ cup Basic Tehina Sauce (see METHOD, page 264)
- 1 bunch scallions, finely chopped
- ½ cup finely chopped dill
- 1 to 1½ teaspoons salt
- 8 slices toasted whole wheat bread, for serving

• Place the peeled eggs in a medium bowl.

• Stir in the amba and Basic Tehina Sauce until evenly coated, mashing the eggs to your desired texture.

• Stir in the scallions and dill and mix well. Season with salt.

• Make sandwiches with the whole wheat toast.

METHOD

Hard-Cooked Egg Wisdom

• Always start with cold water.

• Place the eggs in a saucepan and cover with cold water by a few inches. Bring to a boil and cook at a hard boil for 1 minute. Turn off the heat and cover for 10 minutes.

• With a slotted spoon, remove the eggs from the pot and transfer to a bowl of cold water to help stop the cooking.

4.

"It's time to reconsider cauliflower.
People think it's a watery vegetable.
I consider it a rock star!" —*MIKE*

Vegetables

Butternut Squash Baba Ganoush
with Pomegranate Seeds & Pepitas

Makes 4 servings

Baba ganoush is traditionally made with eggplant, but the combination of roasted vegetable and creamy tehina is too good to dedicate to just one produce item. At Laser Wolf, we use grilled kale for an irresistibly smoky version. Here we use the ubiquitous-for-good-reason butternut squash, but this is a perfect opportunity to experiment with the fun squash varieties that show up in the market before Halloween (kabocha, honeynut, crookneck, Blue Hubbard—just save spaghetti squash and other stringy varieties for another dish!). The addition of pomegranate and toasted pumpkin seeds make this dip a fall fantasy.

> "Steve is so much better at this than I am . . . he's so much more patient!" —*MIKE*

- 2 pounds butternut squash
- ¼ cup olive oil
- 1 teaspoon salt
- 1 cup Basic Tehina Sauce (see METHOD, page 264)
- 1 pomegranate, seeded (see page 67 for Steve's seed-removal trick)
- ½ cup pepitas, toasted in a dry skillet

- Preheat the oven to 425°F.
- Cut the squash in half lengthwise and remove the seeds.
- With the tip of a sharp knife, score the insides of the squash in a crosshatch pattern, then slather the cut sides generously with the oil and season with the salt.
- Roast cut side up until very tender, about 90 minutes. You may notice the flesh separating from the skin.
- When cool to the touch, scoop out the flesh and transfer to a large bowl. You'll need about 2 cups squash; save any leftover squash for another recipe.
- Stir in the Basic Tehina Sauce until it's nice and creamy and evenly mixed.
- Scatter the pomegranate seeds and pepitas on top. Serve with pita or your favorite cracker.

Lucas Solomonov, opposite, at home in the kitchen with his dad, prepping butternut squash. Above, roasted squash scooped from its skins, ready for baba ganoush.

Delicata Squash
with Feta & Hazelnuts

Makes 4 to 6 servings

This is a simple yet sophisticated dish that's easy to throw together on the fly. The skin on delicata squash is totally edible and provides a nice textural contrast to the soft flesh, so leave it on during cooking.

- 2 delicata squash, about 1 pound each
- Olive oil, for roasting and serving
- Salt, for seasoning
- ½ cup pepitas
- ½ cup hazelnuts, preferably skinless
- ½ cup feta cheese, preferably Bulgarian
- Za'atar and Aleppo pepper, for finishing

- Preheat the oven to 425°F.
- Cut the squash, skin on, into rings about ½ inch thick. Remove the seeds.
- Arrange the squash rings in a single layer on a sheet pan. Drizzle the olive oil over the squash and generously season with salt.
- Roast until extremely tender, about 40 minutes.
- While the squash roasts, brown the pepitas in a small skillet over medium heat with about a teaspoon of oil. Stir to coat the seeds and toast until golden, about 2 minutes. Transfer to a small bowl.
- Add the hazelnuts to the pan, no additional oil needed. Stir frequently to evenly toast; the nuts will deepen in color and become aromatic. Transfer to a kitchen towel and cover for a few minutes. If the nuts have skins, they'll easily rub off. Roughly chop the nuts.
- Set the oven to the high broiler setting. Broil the squash to deepen its color, about 2 minutes.
- Crumble the feta and scatter all over the squash right in the pan. Scatter the seeds and chopped nuts on top. Finish with a dusting of the spices and a final drizzle of olive oil.

"We fell in love with the broiler during Covid lockdown. We cooked every day and compared." —*MIKE*

"I'd err on the side of a hotter oven. Most home ovens are just not hot enough." —*MIKE*

Romanian Eggplant with Garlic Confit

Makes 4 to 6 servings

The simplicity of this preparation highlights the sweetness and depth of this often-misunderstood vegetable. We cook the eggplant whole to preserve its beautiful pale color and then season it with garlic that has mellowed and caramelized in a bath of olive oil. It's the garlic that makes this dish "Romanian." Serve as a dip to eat with pita.

- ½ cup olive oil
- 2 medium globe eggplants
- ½ cup Garlic Confit (see METHOD, page 172)
- ¾ teaspoon salt
- Smoked paprika, for finishing
- ½ cup finely chopped parsley
- ½ lemon for finishing
- Sliced cucumber and lettuce leaves, for serving

• Preheat the oven to 425°F.

• Rub the olive oil all over the eggplants and place them on a sheet pan. Roast until extremely tender and collapsing, about 75 minutes.

• Allow the eggplants to cool; this might take 15 minutes or so.

• When cool enough to touch, slice the eggplants in half lengthwise. Scoop out the flesh and transfer it to a large bowl.

• Spoon the garlic confit on top of the eggplant flesh and add enough of the cooked oil from the confit to moisten. Add the salt and mash with a fork into a slightly chunky mixture.

• Spoon the eggplant—mashed garlic mixture onto a serving dish and sprinkle smoked paprika over the top. With a paring knife, make a crosshatch pattern to create little valleys, and spoon more garlic oil on top.

• Scatter the parsley on top of the eggplant, then add a squeeze (or three) of lemon.

• Serve at room temperature with the cucumber and lettuce leaves and fresh bread or pita.

METHOD

Garlic Confit

Makes 1 cup

Leftover garlic oil (without the garlic) can be sealed, refrigerated, and used in salad dressing or pasta sauce within a few days.

- 1 head garlic, cloves peeled and separated
- 1 cup olive oil

- In a small saucepan (the smaller the better), add the garlic and enough oil to cover.
- Set over low heat and gently cook, uncovered, until soft, about 20 minutes.
- Remove from the heat and cover for 5 minutes.
- Spoon the garlic cloves from the oil into a bowl and and mash with a fork.

Broiled Eggplant à la Sabich

Makes 6 servings

We've deconstructed sabich—our favorite pita sandwich—into a robust and beautiful composed dish. Eggplant for sabich is always fried, but here we let the broiler do the hard work to bring out the deep, meaty flavors in the vegetable. You can't have sabich without amba, the Iraqi fermented mango condiment. But a little goes a long way, so we stir it into Basic Tehina Sauce to keep it from completely taking over. This dish is best in the summer when heirloom eggplant varieties start popping up at the market alongside local tomatoes.

- 2 large globe eggplants, peeled and cut into ½-inch rounds
- Salt
- Neutral oil, such as canola, for brushing
- 2 tablespoons olive oil
- 2 teaspoons amba
- 1 cup Basic Tehina Sauce (see METHOD, page 264)
- 4 scallions, thinly sliced into rings
- 3 or 4 hard-cooked eggs (see METHOD, page 160), quartered
- Tomatoes, cut into wedges
- 6 to 8 parsley leaves, stemmed

• Season the eggplant rounds with salt and let sit for about 30 minutes. Rinse well, then squeeze out the water by hand.

• Set the oven to the low broiler setting.

• Arrange the eggplant slices in a single layer on a sheet pan and brush the tops with neutral oil. Broil, checking for progress every 5 minutes until the eggplant is both tender and a deeply roasted color. This could take up to 30 minutes. It's worth the trouble!

• Meanwhile, make the sauce: In a small bowl, stir together the olive oil and 1 teaspoon of the amba. In another bowl, add the Basic Tehina Sauce, stirring in a dollop (1 teaspoon to start) of amba. A little does go a long way, so go easy at first.

• To assemble: Transfer the eggplant slices to a platter and spoon some of the sauce on top.

• Sprinkle the scallions all over, arrange the hard-cooked eggs and tomato wedges on top, and season with salt. Finish with the parsley leaves.

Eggplant & Celery Root Moussaka

with Tripolitan Tomato Sauce

Makes 6 hearty servings

This kitchen project requires two or three days of advanced planning, including weighting the moussaka overnight to compress the layers. But we can't think of a better way to while away some winter hours than in the warmth of a baharat-scented kitchen. The payoff for your patience is a vegetarian moussaka that's every bit as rich and decadent as one with meat.

FOR THE EGGPLANT

- 2 large globe eggplants, peeled
- 1 teaspoon salt
- Neutral oil, for brushing

• Trim the eggplants at both ends. Slice lengthwise into ½-inch-thick pieces. Sprinkle the salt on top and let sit for about 30 minutes to drain the water.

• Rinse the eggplant well and squeeze the rinsed slices by hand to remove as much water as possible.

• Arrange the eggplant slices in a single layer on a broiler-friendly pan. Brush the tops with oil. Set the broiler to low and place the pan right under the element. Broil until the eggplant is deeply caramelized, about 30 minutes. Cool completely.

• The eggplant can be cooked a day in advance; just stack and refrigerate the broiled slices in an airtight container.

BAHARAT BÉCHAMEL

- ½ medium onion, finely chopped
- 4 tablespoons (½ stick) unsalted butter, cut into tablespoon-size pieces
- 1½ teaspoons salt
- 3 tablespoons all-purpose flour
- 1 teaspoon baharat
- 1½ cups whole milk

• In a medium saucepan set over low heat, add the onion, butter, and salt. Cook until the onion has begun to soften, about 5 minutes.

• Stir in the flour, cooking until a paste forms. Sprinkle in the baharat. Whisk in the milk, cooking and whisking constantly for about 10 minutes until the sauce thickens. This sauce is thicker than a usual béchamel sauce.

• Remove from the heat and let cool.

Andrew Henshaw, our chef-partner at Laser Wolf, developed this recipe and shows us how it's done.

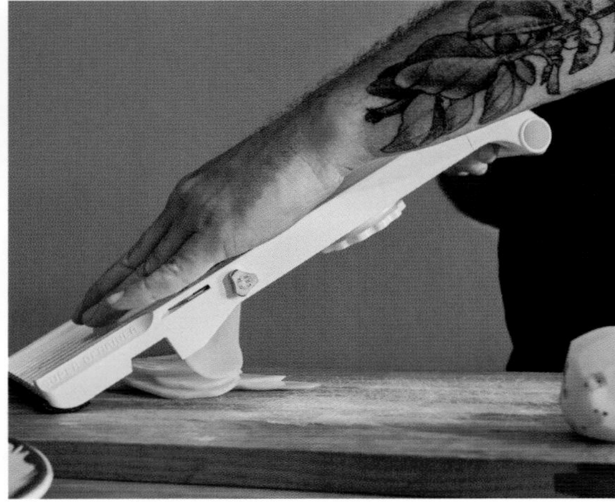

Making: Eggplant & Celery Root Moussaka

We recommend using a mandoline to slice the celery root and potatoes. You can also use the slicer attachment on a food processor. Use one or two small or medium baking dishes, at least two inches deep.

BAKING & MOLDING

- Unsalted butter, for the pan
- 3 medium Yukon potatoes, peeled and sliced into ⅛-inch-thick pieces
- Salt, for seasoning
- 1 medium celery root, peeled and sliced into ¼-inch-thick pieces
- Baharat, for dusting
- 1½ cups grated kashkaval cheese (or provolone)
- 1 cup Tripolitan Tomato Sauce (see METHOD, page 180)

• Generously butter the baking dish (or dishes).

• Preheat the oven to 375°F.

• Cover the bottom of the dish with a layer of potatoes, arranged in an overlapping shingle fashion. Lightly season with salt.

• For the next layer, arrange some of the celery root the same way. Lightly season with salt and dust with baharat.

"Without the overnight compression, this dish would be a hot mess."—*STEVE*

- Spoon on enough béchamel to cover the celery root.
- Sprinkle half of the cheese on top of the béchamel.
- Top with half of the eggplant slices, arranged side by side.
- Repeat all five layers in the same order.
- Lay parchment paper directly on top of the eggplant, pressing down snugly. Wrap the entire dish with aluminum foil.
- Bake until the middle is paring-knife tender, about 1 hour 45 minutes.
- Remove the foil and cool completely. Keep the parchment covering in place.
- Weight the moussaka with cans or dishes on top to compress the layers. Refrigerate overnight.
- When ready to serve, preheat the oven to 350°F. Remove the weights on top. Reheat the moussaka with its parchment cover until warmed through, about 1 hour.
- Remove the parchment. Set the oven to the broiler setting. Broil until the top layer is brown, 2 to 3 minutes.
- Slice and serve with Tripolitan Tomato Sauce.

METHOD

Tripolitan Tomato Sauce

Makes about 1 cup

Inspired by the Jewish cooking of Tripoli, Libya, we love the way that ginger and baharat turn something as familiar as tomato sauce into something new and thrillingly exotic.

- 4 tablespoons (½ stick) unsalted butter
- ½ medium onion, finely chopped
- 2 garlic cloves, thinly sliced
- 1 heaping tablespoon grated fresh ginger
- ½ teaspoon baharat
- 1½ cups crushed tomatoes (from a 15-ounce can)

• Melt the butter in a medium skillet set over medium heat. Add the onion, garlic, and ginger, cooking until softened and fragrant, about 5 minutes. Stir frequently to keep from sticking.

• Add the baharat, stirring until the vegetables are evenly coated.

• Add the tomatoes and their juices, reducing slightly. When the sauce turns rusty red, it's ready.

Cauliflower Chraime

Makes 4 hearty servings

Chraime, an intensely flavored North African fish stew, is traditionally made with fish. But we love it with cauliflower and other vegetables, too. It's traditionally made on the Sabbath because it can be cooked in advance and served at room temperature. The tomato-pepper base is a conserva of sorts, floating in oil, which helps prevent the fish from drying out. The sauce is meant to be aromatic and gutsy, and would be great with sunchokes or Romanesco cauliflower, too. It's also excellent tossed with pasta or served over rice or couscous.

- 1 cup olive oil
- 1 large onion, diced
- 1 red bell pepper, diced
- 6 to 8 garlic cloves, depending on size, thinly sliced
- Scant 1 cup crushed tomatoes (from a 15-ounce can)
- 1 large head cauliflower, cut into florets
- ½ cup stemmed and roughly chopped cilantro
- ¼ cup harissa
- Salt, for seasoning
- ½ lemon, for finishing

• Put the oil and onion in a large skillet set over medium-low heat. Add the pepper and garlic, stirring until evenly mixed. Cook until the onion is really soft, about 30 minutes.

• Add the tomatoes and their juices, cauliflower, half of the cilantro, and the harissa, stirring until evenly coated. Sprinkle with salt.

• Cover and cook over medium-low heat until the cauliflower is fork-tender, about 30 minutes.

• Sprinkle the remaining cilantro on top and add a squeeze of lemon just before serving, either hot or at room temperature.

"Chraime is the kind of thing you'd eat out of the fridge at 2 a.m. Or toss with spaghetti. Killer!" —*MIKE*

Yemenite Cauliflower Wedges
with Schug Labneh

Makes 4 servings

Cauliflower marries beautifully (literally and figuratively) with hawaij, the Yemenite spice blend of cumin, black pepper, and turmeric that turns its subjects a lovely golden color. The schug labneh is the perfect accompaniment—a balance between the blow-your-head-off heat of the chile paste and the cooling power of rich, tangy dairy.

- ½ cup olive oil
- 1 head cauliflower, cut into 6 or 8 wedges, depending on size, with stem intact if possible
- 1 head garlic, skin on, cut in half through the root
- 2 teaspoons salt
- 1 tablespoon hawaij
- 1 cup labneh
- 2 tablespoons Schug (see METHOD, page 58)

• Preheat the oven to 425° F.

• Coat the bottom of a baking dish with half of the olive oil.

• Put the cauliflower into the dish, tucking in the halves of garlic head. It's okay to be snug.

• Pour the remaining oil on top, making sure the cauliflower is well-coated.

• Generously sprinkle the salt and hawaij over the cauliflower. Roast until the cauliflower is paring-knife tender, about 30 minutes.

• While the cauliflower roasts, stir together the labneh and schug in a small bowl. Serve alongside the cauliflower as a dip.

Steamed Broccolini
with Crispy Garlic Sauce

Makes 4 servings

Microwave steaming is magic—it's fast, clean, and effective. If you can't get your hands on Broccolini, choy sum, a thin-stalked relative in the *Brassica* family, or baby bok choy is great, too, as is plain old broccoli.

- 2 bunches Broccolini, about 1 pound
- ½ cup water
- 1 teaspoon salt
- 1 preserved lemon
- 4 garlic cloves, thinly sliced
- ½ cup pine nuts (or unsalted pistachios)
- ½ cup olive oil
- ½ cup packed stemmed and chopped parsley

• Place the Broccolini in a microwave-friendly dish. Pour in the water and scatter the salt on top. Cover with plastic wrap. Steam in 2-minute increments until tender yet still with a little bite.

• Make the sauce: Halve and scrape out the pulp of the preserved lemon. (Store the pulp in the fridge and use it with oil in a salad dressing.)

• Finely chop the preserved lemon rind.

• In a medium skillet set over medium heat, add the garlic, nuts, and olive oil and cook until the nuts are browned and the garlic is crispy. Stir in the parsley and the chopped lemon rind until evenly mixed.

• Arrange the steamed Broccolini on a plate or platter. Spoon the sauce on top.

"Steaming green vegetables
in the microwave is pretty awesome." —*MIKE*

“We caramelize the onion to cook out the water and dress the greens.” —*MIKE*

Olesh-Style Bok Choy

Makes 4 servings

Finally, the answer to all that watery bok choy in your farm share box! "Olesh" is the Arabic word for the chicory that grows in Israel, similar to endive frisée, and it benefits from braising. A long, slow cooking evaporates the excess moisture from the bok choy; the caramelized onions intensify the sweet, earthy flavors. Napa cabbage, chard, or even cauliflower greens would all be great here.

- Olive oil
- 1 large onion, thinly sliced into half-moons
- ½ teaspoon salt
- 1 bunch mature bok choy, thoroughly rinsed

• Set a large skillet over medium heat and coat the bottom with olive oil. Add the onion and the salt. Cook, stirring frequently, until very soft and caramelized, about 30 minutes (see Caramelized Onions, page 38).

• While the onion cooks, prepare the bok choy: Cut the leafy tops into a chiffonade and finely chop some of the stalks (you won't use all of them).

• Stir in the bok choy until evenly coated with oil. Reduce the heat to low and cook until the greens have softened, reduced, and deepened in color. This can take 45 minutes, and even up to an hour.

• Serve the greens piled high in a shallow bowl.

Cabbage Cacio e Pepe

Makes 4 servings

Having a pizza stone in the oven makes such a difference—the bottom of the cabbage gets caramelized, too. The name—cacio e pepe, cheese and pepper—says it all: If this recipe can't convert a cabbage hater, nothing can. Save the trimmings for braised cabbage or borscht.

- 1 medium head green cabbage (about 2 pounds), trimmed as needed
- ¾ teaspoon salt
- ½ cup olive oil
- ½ cup red wine vinegar or distilled white vinegar
- 1 teaspoon coarsely ground black pepper
- 1 cup grated pecorino cheese, plus more if you like

• Preheat the oven to 425°F.

• Slice the cabbage into 4 round slabs about 1 inch thick.

• Arrange the cabbage slices in a nonreactive baking dish or on a sheet pan, preferably one with sides. Sprinkle the salt over the cabbage.

• In a small bowl, stir together the olive oil and vinegar. Pour all over the cabbage slices. Sprinkle the black pepper on top.

• Roast the cabbage slices until paring-knife tender, about 30 minutes. On the oven's broiler setting, broil the cabbage until the tops are very brown (this takes longer than you think it should).

• Remove the cabbage from the broiler and finish with a snowfall of cheese if desired. It's fun to eat the roasted cabbage with a knife and fork.

"The cheese we ate while cooking costs more than the dish!" —*MIKE*

Cabbage with Amba & Tomatoes

Makes 4 servings

The umami-rich combination of amba and tomatoes adds a sweet-and-sour vibe to silky braised cabbage.

- 2 tablespoons olive oil
- ½ large onion, thinly sliced into half-moons
- 1 teaspoon salt, plus more to taste
- 4 cups roughly chopped green cabbage
- 1 cup crushed tomatoes (from a 15-ounce can)
- 4 teaspoons amba
- ½ lemon, for squeezing

• Coat the bottom of a large skillet with the olive oil. Over medium heat, add the onion and salt, cooking until softened, about 10 minutes.

• Add the cabbage, stirring until evenly coated. Cook until the cabbage is translucent, about 5 minutes.

• Stir in the tomatoes with their juices and the amba. Cover and reduce the heat to low. Cook until the cabbage is tender, about 30 minutes.

• Let cool to room temperature; the flavors will deepen as the cabbage cools. Squeeze the lemon over the top. Taste for salt.

Twice-Baked Sweet Potatoes
with Labneh

Makes 4 servings

Our children don't cry out for "real" potatoes when we serve them these. We love countering sugary sweet potatoes with creamy labneh and a savory blast of Parmigiano, black pepper, and scallions.

- 2 sweet potatoes, about 1 pound each
- Olive oil, for slathering
- 1½ teaspoons salt, plus more for seasoning
- ½ cup labneh
- ½ teaspoon ground black pepper
- 2 bunches scallions, white and green parts, finely chopped (1 cup)
- Grated Parmigiano-Reggiano cheese
- Chives, finely chopped, for finishing

• Preheat the oven to 425°F.

• Slather the sweet potatoes with olive oil and season with salt. Place in a baking dish and roast until very soft, about 90 minutes. Keep the oven on.

• Let the potatoes cool slightly, then halve lengthwise.

• When the potatoes are cool enough to touch, scoop out the flesh into a medium bowl. Take care not to pierce the skin/shell of the sweet potato; it's okay to leave some sweet potato flesh behind.

• Add the labneh, salt, black pepper, and scallions to the bowl, stirring until evenly mixed.

• Carefully spoon the mixture into the sweet potato shells. Top with lots of grated cheese.

• Return the pan to the oven and reheat until the sweet potatoes are warmed through, about 20 minutes.

• Set the oven to the broiler setting and broil until the cheesy tops are browned.

• Sprinkle with chives and serve.

"Add more more Parmigiano?" —*STEVE*

"Actually, Steve, I think not." —*MIKE*

Roasted Carrots
with Orange Juice & Pomegranate Molasses

Makes 4 servings

The trick is to cook these carrots so that the liquid is almost evaporated by the time they are done. The remaining orange and pomegranate reduction will glaze the carrots to a beautiful shine and allow the crunchy peanut mixture to stick to their tender surface.

- 1 pound carrots, trimmed as needed, large ones halved lengthwise
- ½ cup orange juice
- 2 tablespoons pomegranate molasses
- ¾ teaspoon salt, plus more for seasoning
- ½ teaspoon ground black pepper
- Pinch Aleppo pepper
- 2 tablespoons olive oil, for drizzling
- 2 tablespoons raw peanuts
- 1 tablespoon coriander seeds
- 1 teaspoon sesame seeds

- Preheat the oven to 425°F.
- Arrange the carrots in a large baking dish or pan.
- In a small bowl, stir together the orange juice, pomegranate molasses, salt, black pepper, and Aleppo pepper.
- Drizzle the olive oil over the carrots until well-coated. Gradually pour the juice mixture on top.
- Roast until the carrots are fork-tender, about 40 minutes, stirring occasionally to make sure all sides are coated in the glaze.
- While the carrots roast, make the peanut topping: In a small skillet, quickly toast the peanuts and coriander seeds. Stir in the sesame seeds, briefly toasting. Season with a pinch or two of salt.
- Set the oven to the broiler setting. Broil the roasted carrots until deeply brown on top.
- Spoon the peanut-seed mixture on top and serve.

"Here's what you can do with those fresh greenmarket carrots." —*MIKE*

TO EACH OTHER
WYLD
CALIFORNIA

Hanging out in the kitchen; from right, Asima Ahmad, Mike's wife, with Mike and sons Lucas and David, and Lizzy Janssen, keeping the adorable Wolfie from the hors d'oeuvres.

Stir-Fried Sugar Snap Peas
with Harissa

Makes 4 servings

This homage to Szechuan stir-fry uses harissa to bring the heat. It really goes a long way to wake up these vegetables. Adding the oil on top of the vegetables in the pan will help minimize spattering. Make sure you have all your veggies prepped before you start cooking.

- 4 cups sugar snap peas (or snow peas or snap beans), trimmed
- 2 celery ribs, thinly sliced
- 1 cup sweet peppers, preferably multicolored, sliced into rings
- 2 tablespoons neutral oil, such as canola
- Salt, for seasoning
- 4 scallions, white and green parts separated and finely chopped
- 1 1-inch piece fresh ginger, finely chopped
- 1 garlic clove, thinly sliced
- 2 tablespoons harissa
- 1 teaspoon sesame seeds
- ½ lime, for finishing

• To a large skillet or wok set over high heat, add the snap peas, celery, and peppers. Pour the oil on top, quickly tossing until the vegetables are evenly coated. Season with salt.

• Add the scallion whites, ginger, and garlic, quickly tossing until coated.

• Add the harissa, tossing for a few minutes until the vegetables are softened and well-coated.

• Scatter the sesame seeds on top. Finish with the scallion greens and a squeeze or two of lime.

"Yes, you *do* need to top, tail, and string the sugar snap peas!" —*STEVE*

Poached Kohlrabi
with Garlic, Dill & Sumac

Makes 4 servings

An underrated vegetable if ever there was one, kohlrabi is a mild and sweet *Brassica* with a pleasing, firm texture. We poach the bulbous stem in water, vinegar, and aromatics until tender and then cook the greens in the same liquid—a real "old country" way of using the whole ingredient.

- 3 kohlrabi (a total of 1½ to 2 pounds), greens removed and reserved
- ½ cup apple cider vinegar
- 2 teaspoons salt
- ½ bunch dill
- 1 small head garlic, cloves separated, skin on
- Coarse salt, for finishing
- 1 teaspoon coriander seeds
- 2 teaspoons ground sumac

• Put the kohlrabi (but not the greens), vinegar, salt, dill, and garlic into a medium saucepan. Add enough cold water to just cover the kohlrabi.

• Bring just to a boil. Cover and cook over medium-low heat until the kohlrabi is paring-knife tender, about 1 hour.

• Remove the kohlrabi from the pan and reserve the cooking liquid.

• Add the reserved greens to the liquid in the pot and cook until tender, about 30 minutes. Remove and finely chop the greens, then transfer them to a platter.

• When the kohlrabi bulbs are cool to the touch, cut into wedges and peel using a paring knife. Arrange on top of the greens. Sprinkle with coarse salt, the coriander seeds, and the sumac. Serve warm or at room temperature.

Shira's Potato Kugel

Makes 6 servings

Shira Rudavsky, Steve's wife, has made this kugel for years (with a little help from Gil Marks, who literally wrote the *Encyclopedia of Jewish Food*). Now the kids—the twins, Eva, below, and Danny, and their big sister, Sally, are into it (but not sixteen-year-old Leo! Too cool for school!). You can use the grater attachment of your food processor to process the potatoes and onion, but we like the texture (and the hands-on experience!) a box grater gives.

- 6 medium or 4 large Yukon potatoes (russets are okay, too)
- 1 large onion
- ½ cup neutral oil, such as canola
- 3 large eggs
- 1½ teaspoons salt
- ½ teaspoon ground black pepper
- ½ bunch parsley, stemmed and finely chopped
- ½ cup stemmed and finely chopped dill
- 6 scallions, finely chopped
- ⅓ cup all-purpose flour

• Preheat the oven to 375°F.

• Into a large bowl, grate the potatoes and onion. Make sure to drain off any residual liquid.

• Put an 8- or 9-inch baking dish in the oven for 5 minutes to preheat.

• Carefully pour ¼ cup of the oil into the pan while it is still in the oven and let it heat until the oil shimmers, about 10 minutes.

• In a medium bowl, whisk the eggs. Add to the potato-onion mixture, stirring until everything is evenly coated. Add the salt, black pepper, parsley, dill, scallions, flour, and the remaining ¼ cup of oil. Stir until evenly mixed.

• Fill the preheated dish and bake until golden brown and bubbly, about 1 hour.

Potter
AND THE
STONE

Steve, opposite, prefers to grate potatoes by hand, with Danny. Sally, above, helps Shira with the seasoning.

Phyllo Borekas
with Swiss Chard & Feta

Makes 2 large borekas, or about 2 dozen pieces

Working with phyllo dough can be intimidating, but we endorse a "fake it till you make it" approach because this dish is so good and far easier than it looks. Just remember to keep the phyllo sheets covered when you're not working with them. Any tears will disappear once you roll it all up.

- 1 bunch multicolored chard, stems separated from the leaves
- 2 tablespoons olive oil
- ½ large onion, diced
- 4 garlic cloves, thinly sliced
- 1 teaspoon salt
- 1 cup feta cheese
- 4 sheets phyllo dough, thawed
- 5 tablespoons unsalted butter, melted, for brushing

MAKE THE FILLING

• Cut the chard stems into a small dice. Cut the leaves into ribbonlike strips.

• In a large skillet over medium heat, add the oil, then the diced chard stems, onion, and garlic, turning the vegetables until evenly coated. Add the salt and cook until the vegetables are softened, about 5 minutes.

• Add the chard leaves, turning until well-coated in oil. Cook until visibly reduced, about 3 minutes.

• Remove the pan from the heat and let cool. Drain off any residual liquid.

• Transfer the chard to a bowl and stir in the feta until evenly mixed.

ASSEMBLY & BAKING

• Preheat the oven to 400°F.

• Working with one phyllo sheet at a time, keeping the other sheets covered with a damp towel, lay the first phyllo sheet on a work surface and brush with melted butter.

• Cover with a second sheet, repeating with a coat of melted butter. Keep the remaining sheets (for the second boreka) covered while you work.

• Leaving a 2-inch border, carefully spoon half of the filling along the long side closest to you. Gradually roll the dough away from you into a giant cigar.

• Starting at one end, shape the roll into a coil. Carefully arrange in a cake pan or an ovenproof skillet. Brush the top with butter. Repeat for the second boreka, and wrap it around the first.

• Bake until golden brown, about 40 minutes. Cool slightly, carefully remove the coil from the pan with a spatula, and cut into 2-inch pieces to serve.

"We use butter on the phyllo dough
because there's cheese in the stuffing."—MIKE

Making: Phyllo Borekas with Swiss Chard & Feta

Brushing the phyllo layers with melted butter helps make them flaky in the oven. But it also keeps the sheets hydrated to prevent cracking during the rolling and coiling stages.

METHOD

Phyllo Tips

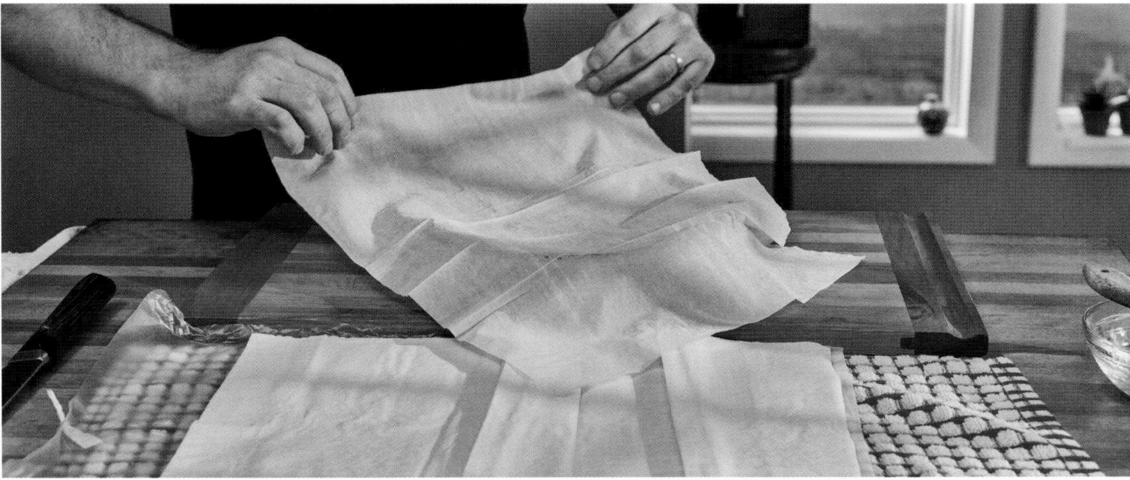

"Be really diligent about keeping the dough covered." —MIKE

- Before you can work with it, the phyllo dough must be completely thawed, preferably overnight in the refrigerator.
- To thaw at room temperature, remove the dough from the box, carefully unroll, and lay the sheets on a flat surface between two damp towels for about an hour.
- Always work with just one layer at a time, keeping the other sheets covered with the damp towel.

Mushroom Phyllo Cigars with Honey

Makes about 16 pieces

The inspiration for this dish started with an idea for a savory baklava. A concentrated mushroom duxelles is rolled into little phyllo cigars and then drizzled with honey while still warm. These can be stored unbaked in your freezer and then popped directly in the oven when unexpected guests arrive.

- 2 tablespoons olive oil
- 4 garlic cloves, minced
- 1 pound button or cremini mushrooms, diced small
- 1½ tablespoons red wine vinegar
- 1 teaspoon salt
- ½ cup finely chopped dill
- ½ cup finely chopped parsley
- 2 phyllo sheets, thawed
- Neutral oil, such as canola, for brushing
- ¼ cup sesame seeds, for topping
- Honey, for drizzling

MAKE THE FILLING

• Coat the bottom of a large skillet set over medium-high heat with the olive oil. Add the garlic, then the mushrooms, stirring, until the mushrooms are soft and brown, about 15 minutes.

• Add the vinegar and the salt, turning up the heat, and cook until the vinegar is evaporated, about 10 minutes. Let cool.

• Spread the mushrooms on a board, add the herbs, and chop into a very fine mince. Transfer to a medium bowl.

ASSEMBLY & BAKING

• Preheat the oven to 400°F.

• Working with one phyllo sheet at a time (keeping the other sheet covered with a damp towel), lay the first phyllo sheet on a work surface and brush with the neutral oil.

• Cover with the second sheet and brush with a coat of oil. Press lightly on top to make sure the dough remains flat.

• Leaving a 1-inch border, spoon half of the filling in a thin line along one edge of the long side of the sheet, top to bottom.

• With the tip of a sharp knife, slice the sheet down the middle to make a second roll.

• Spoon on the remaining filling the same way, along the left side of the second sheet, leaving a 1-inch border.

• From the left edges, roll each sheet into a very snug log.

• Cut each log into smaller pieces, about 1½ inches long, and gently place them on a baking pan.

• Brush neutral oil on top of the rolls, then sprinkle on the sesame seeds. Bake for about 20 minutes, until the phyllo is crisp and slightly browned.

• Serve, preferably warm, with a drizzle of honey on the top.

Making: Mushroom Phyllo Cigars with Honey

"You've got to think of cooking as a cumulative process. Pace yourself. You're playing the long game!"*—MIKE*

Take care to roll the cigars snugly so that the filling won't fall out when baked (but not too snugly or the dough will tear!).

Phyllo Quiche
with Summer Squash

Makes 6 hearty servings

Using premade phyllo sheets is much easier than rolling out pie dough, but the result is just as impressive. A preheated baking steel or sheet pan helps alleviate the dreaded soggy bottom crust. Make sure to drain off any excess liquid from the squash before placing it in the phyllo.

- 4 medium yellow straight-neck summer squash and/or zucchini (about 2 pounds), sliced into rounds about ¼ inch thick
- 2 tablespoons olive oil
- 2 teaspoons salt
- 4 eggs
- 1 cup whole milk
- ¼ teaspoon ground black pepper
- 1½ cups grated kashkaval cheese (or provolone)
- Neutral oil, for brushing
- 4 phyllo sheets, thawed

• In a large bowl, stir together the squash, olive oil, and 1 teaspoon of the salt until evenly coated.

• Arrange in a single layer on a sheet pan.

• Set the oven to the broiler setting and cook until the squash is tender and the tops are brown, about 10 minutes.

• In a medium bowl, beat the eggs and the milk, seasoning with the remaining teaspoon of salt and the black pepper. Add the cheese, whisking until evenly mixed.

• Preheat the oven to 350° F. Place a baking steel or sheet pan on the middle rack.

• Assemble the quiche in a 9- or 10-inch pie pan. Brush the bottom and sides of the pan generously with the neutral oil.

• Working with one phyllo sheet at a time (keeping the other sheets covered top and bottom with a damp towel), place the first phyllo sheet into the pan and brush all over with neutral oil.

• Repeat with each phyllo sheet, oiling in between additions.

• Arrange half of the squash on top of the phyllo. Pour half of the egg mixture on top. Then add the remaining squash, being careful to leave the residual liquid behind. Finish with the remaining egg mixture.

• Fold the corner edges of the phyllo over the filling, one quadrant at a time, brushing each layer generously with neutral oil as you go. Brush oil on top and seal like a package.

• Place on the preheated steel or pan and bake until golden on top, about 45 minutes.

• Check for doneness with a paring knife inserted into the middle. The knife should come out clean.

• Let the quiche cool for at least 10 minutes before serving.

"The crosscut on this quiche through all the layers is looking sick!" —*MIKE*

Making: Phyllo Quiche with Summer Squash

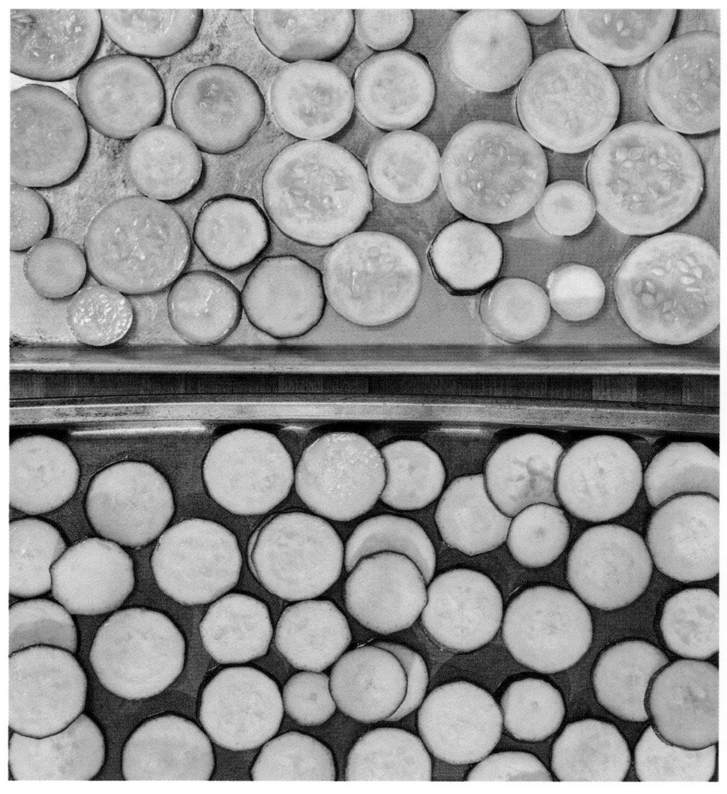

Be sure to have your mise en place ready before you begin assembly. Then work quickly but deliberately; once you add the liquid, there's no turning back.

> "I'm using four layers of phyllo to give it extra strength." —*STEVE*

5.

"A little meat is a good thing
every once in a while.
Just make sure it counts."—*STEVE*

Meat

Montreal Slow-Roasted Short Ribs

Makes 6 servings

The short rib plate might be the best piece of beef a cow has to offer. Found on the lower rib cage next to the brisket and below the prime rib, it's well-marbled and full of beefy flavor. Short ribs are often braised low and slow to break down the connective tissue and yield tender, juicy meat with a luxurious mouthfeel. At our restaurant Abe Fisher, we always smoked the short ribs before the slow roast. It's Texas-barbecue-meets-Jewish-deli.

- 2 tablespoons salt
- 2 teaspoons garlic powder
- 2 teaspoons smoked paprika
- 1 three-bone beef plate (about 4 pounds)
- 2 tablespoons black peppercorns
- 2 tablespoons coriander seeds
- 1 teaspoon allspice berries
- Rye bread, for serving
- Dark mustard, for serving

• In a small bowl, stir together the salt, garlic powder, and smoked paprika. Rub this mix all over the meat.

• Coarsely grind the black peppercorns, coriander seeds, and allspice berries. Stir together and rub all over the fat cap, creating a thick crust.

• Wrap the meat tightly with plastic wrap, paying attention to the fat cap side. The plastic will draw moisture out from the meat to the surface, ensuring that the crust actually sticks to the meat.

• Cure overnight in the refrigerator.

• When ready to cook, preheat the oven to 275° F. Unwrap the meat and place on a sheet pan. Cook, uncovered, for 8 hours. The meat should be extremely tender. Let the meat rest for up to 1 hour.

• Before slicing, gently slide out the bones and discard. Remove the layer of cartilage on the underside of the plate where the bones were. Slice the meat against the grain.

• For each sandwich, slather two slices of rye bread with mustard and pile on slices of meat.

"Short rib meat should be eaten warm. Yank the ribs out of the oven, let 'em rest, then go at 'em!" —*MIKE*

Making: Montreal Slow-Roasted Short Ribs

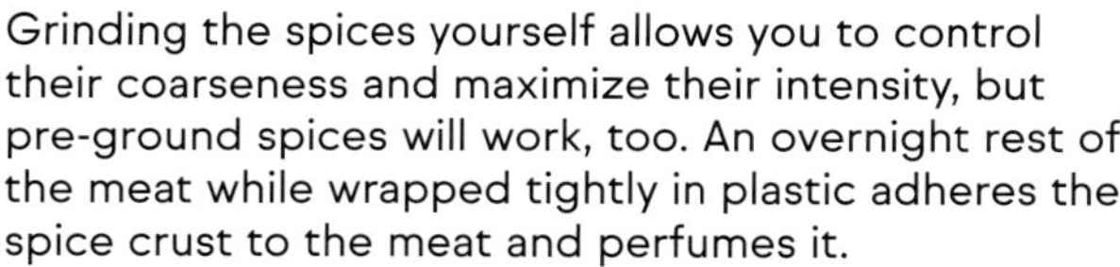

Grinding the spices yourself allows you to control their coarseness and maximize their intensity, but pre-ground spices will work, too. An overnight rest of the meat while wrapped tightly in plastic adheres the spice crust to the meat and perfumes it.

When properly cooked, the short rib bones will slide out cleanly with little resistance. Don't forget the mustard and rye bread!

> "Slow-cooked coriander does something special to meat!" —*MIKE*

"Sliced, with celery root puree and a little black truffle paste? Sick."—*MIKE*

Short Ribs with Amba–Passion Fruit Glaze

Makes 5 to 6 servings

These short ribs are a nod to Kansas City barbecue: The sweet tomato-based sauce is balanced with tart passion fruit juice and the funk of amba, the Iraqi fermented mango condiment. This is one complex, sweet-and-sour, lip-smacking piece of beef. A quick trip under the broiler to caramelize the sauce after cooking takes it up one more notch. This recipe calls for individual bones cut from a three-bone short rib plate—you may need to special-order the cut.

FOR THE SPICE RUB

- 2 tablespoons salt
- 2 teaspoons ground cumin
- 2 teaspoons onion powder
- 2 teaspoons garlic powder
- 1 teaspoon ground black pepper
- 1 three-bone beef plate (about 4 pounds), bones separated

• Stir together the salt and spices in a small bowl and rub all over the meat. Wrap each rib in plastic and cure overnight in the refrigerator.

• When ready to cook, preheat the oven to 275°F and unwrap the meat.

FOR THE BRAISING LIQUID

- 1 cup ketchup
- 1 cup water
- 2 tablespoons amba
- 2 tablespoons brown sugar
- ½ cup passion fruit puree

• Transfer the overnight-cured meat into your favorite Dutch oven (or oven-friendly pot with a lid).

• In a medium bowl, stir together the ketchup, water, amba, brown sugar, and passion fruit puree. Pour over the meat in the pot.

• Cover and make sure the lid can lie flat. Cook until very tender, 5 to 6 hours.

• Uncover and cool completely. Cover and refrigerate overnight.

• The next day, skim the fat off the top.

• Preheat the oven to 350°F.

• Cover and reheat the meat until warmed through, 20 to 25 minutes. Spoon pan sauce over the top and glaze under the broiler for a few minutes.

"We like the decadence of a short rib plate, not those stingy little beef back ribs." —*MIKE*

Za'atar-Rubbed Lamb Chops
with Artichokes, Olives & Potatoes

Makes 4 servings

Lamb chops are the gateway lamb—even folks who are put off by lamb's reputation for gaminess go crazy for these meat lollipops. Lamb and za'atar are a classic pairing—you can just picture Israeli lambs grazing on the wild herbs. We prefer lamb cooked to a rosy medium; it's more tender that way, and our kids send it back less often.

- 1 pound fingerling or Yukon potatoes, halved lengthwise
- 2 tablespoons olive oil
- 2 teaspoons salt
- 2 small racks of lamb (1 to 1¼ pounds each)
- 1 tablespoon za'atar
- 1 16-ounce jar artichoke hearts, drained
- 1 to 2 tablespoons tapenade
- ¼ cup parsley leaves
- ¼ cup mint leaves

• Preheat the oven to 450°F.

• In a medium bowl, stir together the potatoes, olive oil, and ½ teaspoon of the salt. Arrange in a single layer on a sheet pan.

• In a small bowl, stir together the za'atar and the remaining 1½ teaspoons of salt.

• Rub the lamb with the salted za'atar and lay the racks on top of the potatoes.

• Roast for 30 minutes. Remove the meat to rest and return the potatoes to the oven for another 5 minutes.

• Set the oven to the low broiler setting. Place the lamb chops under the broiler to brown on top, 3 to 5 minutes.

• Transfer the potatoes to a medium bowl. Stir in the artichokes and tapenade until evenly mixed. Chop the parsley and mint. Sprinkle on top of the vegetables.

• Rest the lamb for at least 15 minutes, then carve into single or double chops and serve with the vegetables.

Braised Lamb Shanks
with Sour Cherry & Cola

Makes 4 hearty servings

Growing up, we only had soda in the house for "company" (we don't let our kids drink it at home either!). So it feels a little subversive to crack open a can of Coke for this recipe. (Just consider it the non-treyf version of the classic Southern dish of ham glazed with Coca-Cola.) We add sour cherry juice to help curb the sweetness.

This dish is a three-day affair—with very little hands-on time. The shanks are cured overnight with Three C's Spice Blend (see below). After cooking, the shanks are chilled overnight so the meat can absorb the braising liquid and the solidified fat can be easily removed.

- 2½ teaspoons Three C's Spice Blend (stir together 1 teaspoon each ground coriander and ground cumin, ½ teaspoon ground caraway, and a pinch or two ground cardamom)
- 1½ tablespoons salt
- 4 lamb shanks (about 3 pounds total)
- ½ large onion, thinly sliced
- 8 ounces cola
- 8 ounces sour cherry juice

- Mix the Three C's with the salt and rub all over the lamb shanks. Cover the meat with plastic wrap and let cure overnight in the refrigerator.
- When ready to cook, preheat the oven to 275°F.
- Transfer the meat to a Dutch oven or ovenproof pot with a lid. Blanket the meat with the onion. Pour the cola and sour cherry juice into the pot.
- Cover and cook for 4 hours.
- Completely cool before refrigerating.
- The next day, skim the fat and bring the meat to room temperature before cooking.
- Preheat the oven to 350°F.
- Pour the braising liquid into a small saucepan and reduce until slightly thickened.
- Cover the meat and cook until warmed through, about 30 minutes.
- Spoon the reduced sauce over the meat. Switch the oven to the low broiler setting and broil the meat, uncovered, for a minute, just to glaze the sauce.

"It's great to be able to broil in my kitchen
and not set off the smoke alarm!"—MIKE

Coffee-Cardamom Strip Steak
with Shallot Confit

Makes 4 servings

A rub of coffee, cardamom, and black pepper really works magic on a great steak. The Shallot Confit is an excellent accompaniment to steak or anything, really. This is such an easy, elegant date-night dinner — one we fantasize about!

- 2 teaspoons salt
- ½ teaspoon finely ground coffee
- 6 cardamom pods, hulls removed, seeds ground
- ½ teaspoon ground black pepper
- 2 boneless New York strip steaks (about 1 pound each)
- Shallot Confit (see METHOD, right)

• In a small bowl, stir together the salt, coffee, cardamom, and black pepper. Rub all over the steaks. Wrap the meat in plastic and refrigerate to cure overnight (or for a minimum of 2 hours).

• When ready to cook, set the oven to the low broiler setting. Cook the steaks for 4 to 5 minutes per side.

• Let rest for about 10 minutes before serving.

• Serve with the Shallot Confit and its sauce.

METHOD

Shallot Confit

- 3 tablespoons red wine vinegar
- 2 tablespoons date molasses
- ½ cup brewed coffee
- ½ teaspoon salt
- 6 cardamom pods, smashed (about ½ teaspoon)
- 6 shallots, peeled

• Place all the ingredients except the shallots in a medium skillet set over medium heat. Give the pan a few stirs until the sauce is well-mixed.

• Now add the shallots and bring the sauce to a simmer.

• Reduce the heat to medium-low and cook until the shallots are tender, about 1 hour.

Romanian Pan-Fried Skirt Steak
with Seared Romaine

Makes 4 servings

We think there's no more flavorful cut of steak than skirt, but it's thin—so we cook it over high heat so it develops a crust and doesn't overcook on the inside. Skirt steak is a perfect candidate for the "Romanian" treatment: rubbing it with tons of garlic and paprika. With a hot and flavorful skillet already going, we like to sear cut heads of romaine lettuce in the meat drippings.

FOR THE STEAK

- 6 garlic cloves
- 1½ teaspoons salt
- 1 teaspoon smoked paprika
- 1 teaspoon ground black pepper
- 2 tablespoons olive oil
- 1½ pounds skirt steak
- 2 to 4 tablespoons neutral oil, such as canola, or chicken schmaltz, for pan-frying

• Pulverize the garlic with a mortar and pestle or by smearing it with a knife. Add the salt, smoked paprika, and black pepper, working the mixture into a paste. Add the olive oil.

• Rub all over the meat and let marinate for an hour at room temperature.

• When ready to cook, generously coat the bottom of a large skillet with 2 to 4 tablespoons of the neutral oil, depending on the size of the pan.

• Sear the meat on both sides until well-crusted and dark, 3 to 4 minutes per side, depending on how done you like it.

• There may be some spattering, so don't forget to turn on your exhaust fan.

• Transfer the meat to a cutting board to rest. While it rests, sear the romaine.

FOR THE ROMAINE

- 4 romaine hearts
- 1 recipe Tehina Caesar Dressing (page 60)

• Over medium heat in the same skillet used to cook the meat, lay the romaine cut side down.

• Cook until the lettuce is brown and even a little bit charred, about 3 minutes.

• Remove the romaine hearts from the skillet and set on a serving dish.

• Slice the meat and set alongside the romaine. Spoon Tehina Caesar Dressing on top of the lettuce and meat.

"There ought to be a picture of a skirt steak next to the word 'beefy' in the dictionary." —*STEVE*

Making: Romanian Pan-Fried Skirt Steak with Seared Romaine

It's important to pulverize the garlic and seasonings into a paste (we like our mortar and pestle, but a broad knife blade works, too) before rubbing it onto the meat. This makes sure the seasoning adheres to the meat, which will prevent it from burning.

"This is the steak you want after a long day at work. It's got guts! It'll get your blood pumping again." —*STEVE*

Steve's Leg of Lamb with Harissa

Makes 4 or 5 servings

It was five o'clock on a Wednesday: The kids were ravenous, the dinner plans were none, and the food supplies were low. In the fridge was a boneless leg of lamb, a container of cherry tomatoes, and a few bell peppers—left from our weekly Costco shopping trip. A leg of lamb sounds like a weekend project—nothing to mess with this late on a weeknight. But I quickly heated up a Dutch oven and rubbed the leg of lamb with salt and harissa.

While the lamb was searing, I cut up some bell peppers and peeled some garlic. When the lamb was well-browned, I lifted it up with a fork, dumped in the tomatoes, peppers, and garlic, set the lamb on top, and threw it in the oven with a lid. When the lamb was done, I rested it on a cutting board while I returned the tomato-pepper situation to the stovetop to reduce into the most delicious stew.

- 1 boneless leg of lamb (about 3½ pounds), rolled and tied
- 1½ tablespoons salt
- 2 tablespoons harissa
- 1 head garlic, cloves separated and peeled
- 1 pint cherry tomatoes
- 2 red bell peppers, cut into large dice
- ½ bunch parsley, stemmed and chopped

- Preheat the oven to 400°F.
- Make sure the meat fits in a Dutch oven or pot with a lid. Rub the salt and harissa all over the meat. Heat the pot first, then sear the meat until caramelized on all sides, 3 to 4 minutes.
- Lift the meat, then add the garlic, cherry tomatoes, and peppers to the pot.
- Cover and cook until the internal temperature of the meat is about 140°F, 50 to 55 minutes.
- Remove the meat from the pot and let rest.
- Return the pot with the vegetables to the stove over medium heat. Cook until the vegetables have reduced into a chunky sauce, about 10 minutes.
- Remove the string and slice the meat.
- Spoon the sauce onto a platter and arrange the meat on top. Add the parsley just before serving.

"In little more than an hour, I went from a panic to feeling like a hero. Dinner was on the table. And not a bad one at that." —*STEVE*

By cooking the lamb in a sturdy covered casserole—a Dutch oven, opposite—the meat steams and roasts simultaneously. And the hot pot works for sautéing the vegetables after the meat has been removed.

Beef & Sweet Potato Sofrito

Makes 4 or 5 servings

Sofrito is a Sephardic meat and root vegetable stew that likely originated in Jerusalem. "Sofrito" means "prefried," which describes its unusual technique: Root vegetables are fried in oil and removed; the meat is then seared in the same pot. Everything is cooked slowly in a covered casserole (without additional liquid), yielding one of the most guilelessly delicious meat and potatoes dish we've ever had. We like sofrito with sweet potatoes!

- 2 pounds beef chuck, cut into 4-inch chunks
- 2½ teaspoons salt
- 1 teaspoon ground black pepper
- ½ large onion, thinly sliced into half-moons
- 1 head garlic, skin on, sliced crosswise
- ½ cup neutral oil, such as canola
- 2 medium sweet potatoes, skin on, quartered
- 1 tablespoon red wine vinegar

• Season the beef with 2 teaspoons of the salt and the black pepper. Stir in the onion until evenly mixed. Cover and refrigerate overnight.

• Preheat the oven to 375°F.

• In an oven-friendly pot with a lid, stir the garlic and oil together over medium-high heat. Add the sweet potatoes, cut side down, and fry until browned and crusty, about 8 minutes.

• Transfer to a bowl. (A slotted spoon is helpful for retrieving the garlic.) Season with the remaining ½ teaspoon of salt.

• Add the meat to the pot in batches; the flavor comes from searing the chunks on all sides. Add the garlic and sweet potatoes, plus the red wine vinegar. Cover and cook in the preheated oven until the beef is very tender, approximately 2 hours.

"To make sure the meat is well-seasoned, it helps to get in there with your hands." —*MIKE*

METHOD

Kofte Mix

Makes 1½ pounds

This baharat-spiced ground meat mixture is a versatile crowd-pleaser that we use in everything from Red Cabbage Pie (page 248) to Braised Kofte Meatballs with Pomegranate & Sumac (page 246) to Sheet Pan Kebabs (page 254).

It's important to knead the kebab mixture thoroughly to bind the network of proteins in the meat, which holds the kofte together and gives the meatballs or kebabs their trademark sausage-like texture. We add baking soda and club soda to make the kofte puff up during cooking, to give the meat mixture a little bounce. We use a mixer with a paddle attachment for the kneading, but at home it's much more fun to use your (clean) hands!

"Cutting onions fine enough is really hard. It's one of the things I don't miss about culinary school." —*STEVE*

- 1½ pounds ground beef or lamb
- 1 medium onion, very finely chopped
- 1¾ cups very finely chopped parsley (about ¾ bunch)
- 2 teaspoons salt, plus more for seasoning
- 1 teaspoon baharat
- ¼ teaspoon plus ⅛ teaspoon baking soda
- 3 tablespoons club soda

• In a bowl large enough to mix and knead the meat, work the onion and parsley into the mix. Then add the salt, baharat, baking soda, and club soda.

• Use both hands to knead until the mixture looks like sausage. This could take up to 10 minutes.

• Before the meat rests, test it for seasoning and puffiness (a true sign of Ottoman kebabs) by pinching off a spoonful and frying it in a dry skillet until brown on both sides. Now's the time to taste the cooked meat and add seasoning if needed.

• Place plastic wrap directly on top of the meat; this helps minimize oxidation. Then cover the bowl with another layer of wrap. Refrigerate for at least 4 hours.

Braised Kofte Meatballs
with Pomegranate & Sumac

Makes 4 generous servings

This Persian riff on sweet-and-sour meatballs owes its character to bottled pomegranate juice (the sweet) and sumac (the sour). Serve over rice with plenty of dill and a drizzle of Basic Tehina Sauce.

- Olive oil
- 1 recipe Kofte Mix (see METHOD, page 245), shaped into 1-inch balls
- 1 large onion, thinly sliced into half-moons
- 2 tablespoons ground sumac
- 1 cup bottled pomegranate juice
- 1 teaspoon salt
- Basic Tehina Sauce (see METHOD, page 264), for drizzling
- ¼ cup chopped dill, for finishing

• Coat the bottom of a large skillet or saucepan with olive oil. When the oil is hot, drop in the balls, in batches, and brown for a few minutes on all sides. Be careful when turning; they are delicate. Transfer to a plate.

• Add the sliced onion to the skillet, turning to coat. Keep an eye out for stuck-on bits, loosening as needed with a wooden spoon. Cook over medium-low heat until softened, 12 to 15 minutes.

• Stir in the sumac, turning until the onions are evenly coated. Add the pomegranate juice and bring to a boil. Cook, uncovered, until reduced by half. Add the salt.

• Return the meatballs to the pan, allowing the liquid to keep reducing until it looks more like syrup.

• When ready to serve, drizzle on some tehina sauce, and scatter fresh dill on top.

Kofte-Filled Red Cabbage Pie

Makes 8 to 10 servings

We've turned the humble stuffed cabbage into a real presentation piece: a pie! You can use a deep skillet or a round baking dish. Just make sure to wrap it tightly in foil or to use a snug-fitting lid so that the rice can steam and cook completely. And don't forget to photograph the reveal! Serve with Tripolitan Tomato Sauce (page 180) or your favorite marinara sauce.

"Cabbage is the least expensive, most underrated vegetable ever!" —*MIKE*

- 1 large head red cabbage
- Salt
- 1 cup jasmine rice, soaked in water for 30 minutes and rinsed a few times
- 1 recipe Kofte Mix (see METHOD, page 245), refrigerated for at least 4 hours
- 1 cup crushed tomatoes (from a 15-ounce can)
- ½ cup water
- Olive oil

• Peel away and discard any damaged or tough outer leaves of the cabbage. Then carefully remove whole cabbage leaves intact and make a pile.

• Have a medium pot of boiling salted water ready. Drop a few leaves at a time into the water, blanching until the leaves are soft and pliable, about 7 minutes. (The leaves may change color—that's fine.) Remove and let cool.

• In a large bowl, stir the rice, kofte mix, crushed tomatoes, and water until evenly mixed.

• Preheat the oven to 350°F.

• Coat the bottom and sides of the pan with olive oil. Layer the bottom generously with some of the blanched cabbage leaves, overlapping as needed and making sure there is enough of an overhang to cover the top of the pie. Remember to leave room for two layers of the filling; the rice will expand as it cooks.

• Measure out about half of the filling and smooth it on the bottom layer of cabbage. Sprinkle with salt and drizzle with oil.

• Repeat this for another layer: cabbage, kofte filling, salt, and olive oil.

• Fold the hanging cabbage leaves toward the center of the top layer and gently press down with your fingetips. Patch the top with more blanched cabbage leaves as needed.

• Cover tightly with foil or a lid and bake for 90 minutes. Uncover and bake for an additional 10 minutes.

• Cool for at least 30 minutes. Carefully invert and cut into slices.

Goldie

Making: Kofte-Filled Red Cabbage Pie

"I buy big bags of Vietnamese jasmine rice and soak it to wash the starch away." —*MIKE*

"We like to use red cabbage for the look, but any cabbage will do." —*STEVE*

It's important to fully encase the pie in cabbage to keep the steam inside as it cooks, so don't be afraid to overlap the leaves. The bottom of the pie will become the presentation side, so use the nicest leaves to line your cooking vessel and save any smaller or torn pieces for patching the top.

Sheet Pan Kebabs

Yemenite Kebabs

Merguez Kebabs

Kofte Kebabs

Sheet Pan Kebabs

Alton Brown calls the broiler an upside-down grill, and we've grudgingly come to accept this wisdom. The broiler used to be the catchall drawer beneath the oven. But now we line a sheet pan with foil and set the broiler to low, moving the oven rack as close to the element as possible, and broil until the kebabs are cooked through, 5 to 6 minutes total, turning them halfway.

Yemenite Kebabs

Makes 30 to 32 pieces

This brainchild of Laser Wolf chef Andrew Henshaw essentially infuses the flavors of Yemenite soup into a kebab! He created an instant classic.

- ¾ bunch cilantro, stemmed
- 2 pounds ground beef or lamb
- 1 medium onion, finely chopped (about 1½ cups)
- 3 tablespoons soda water or plain seltzer
- 4½ teaspoons hawaij
- 1 tablespoon Schug (see METHOD, page 58)
- 2½ teaspoons salt
- ½ teaspoon baking soda

• Finely chop the cilantro. Place in a large bowl along with the meat, onion, soda water, hawaij, schug, salt, and baking soda.

• Knead thoroughly, for longer than you think, until the mixture looks like sausage. This could take up to 10 minutes.

• Wrap and refrigerate for at least 4 hours.

• Roll the meat into 2-inch chubby logs and place on a parchment-lined sheet pan. Cover and refrigerate to firm up, for at least 1 hour.

Kofte Kebabs

Makes about 24 pieces

Use the Kofte Mix (see Method, page 245) and form individual kebabs. Refrigerate to firm up for at least 1 hour.

Merguez Kebabs

Makes about 35 pieces

Traditionally, merguez is stuffed into lamb casings to create one long, thin sausage. These freestyle cylinders are just as delicious.

- 2 pounds ground lamb
- ⅓ cup stemmed and finely chopped cilantro
- 2½ teaspoons salt
- ½ teaspoon baking soda
- 2½ tablespoons harissa
- 3 tablespoons club soda

• Place all the ingredients in a large bowl. Knead thoroughly, for longer than you think, until the mixture looks like sausage. This could take up to 10 minutes.

• Wrap and refrigerate for at least 4 hours.

• Roll the meat into thin cylinders. Cover and return to the refrigerator to firm up, for at least 1 hour.

Yemenite

Kofte

Merguez

"We know the best kebabs are cooked over charcoal. But light the grill on a Tuesday?" —*STEVE*

We love kebabs! Beef or lamb, flavored with onion or garlic, baharat or hawaij; studded with dill, cilantro, or fresh parsley. We cook kebabs inside or (preferably) outside whenever we can.

K'FAR

6.

"We're cooking every dish from scratch. Nothing fake in this book!" —*STEVE*

Grains

Our Grain Pantry

BELUGA LENTILS

We love these tiny black lentils, "beans," really, named for their resemblance to caviar, because they retain their shape and texture during cooking and thus make a fine stand-in for ground meat in pasta sauces and ragouts. Beluga lentils are an excellent source of plant-based protein with plenty of nutritional benefits, even when compared to other legumes.

PEARL BARLEY

Barley is called "pearl" when it's separated from its hull and polished to remove the bran layer. Like wheat, barley is a grass and contains gluten. Its high fiber content stabilizes blood sugar. Barley is the world's fourth most cultivated grain behind corn, rice, and wheat. Its chewy texture shines in soups and grain salads.

FARRO

Farro can refer to three different wheat varieties: spelt, emmer, and einkorn. It's sold in multiple stages of processing, with varying amounts of husk and bran, each requiring specific cooking methods. But when you master them, farro is delicious and nutritious with a nutty flavor and pleasant chew. Just make sure to follow the cooking instructions on your particular package.

BULGUR

Bulgur is wheat that has been parboiled and cracked. It's a very convenient product to work with, as it does not require cooking, only rehydrating in water. Bulgur is the classic grain in tabbouleh, a main ingredient in kibbeh, and makes a terrific hot breakfast cereal. It's available in different levels of coarseness depending on the recipe and your preferences.

FREEKAH

Freekah is durum wheat that's harvested while still green. To remove the straw and chaff, piles of the wheat are set on fire. High moisture content in the green seeds keeps them from burning and gives freekah its smoky flavor (see Mushroom Freekah Soup, page 112). Freekah is available as a whole grain or cracked (like green bulgur), so follow package cooking instructions.

JASMINE RICE

We like this long-grain, fragrant rice for its versatility and popcorn-like aromas. Jasmine rice is stickier than basmati (another favorite), helpful for dishes like Eggplant T'bit (page 282) and Chicken Maqluba (page 290) where we want the rice to hold its shape when it's unmolded from its cooking vessel. Always rinse the rice thoroughly before using, until the water runs clear.

CHICKPEAS

What can we say? This little bean has been very good to us: hummus!! It's also super nutritious and highly sustainable. The Instant Pot has simplified the prospect of using dried chickpeas, but the canned version is convenient and generally of very good quality.

ISRAELI COUSCOUS

Not actually couscous, these are pearls of dried pasta. We always dry-toast Israeli couscous on a sheet pan in the oven to deepen its flavor before boiling it in salted water. Kids love to spoon it up with tomato sauce. It makes a great addition to soups, and we particularly love it cooked risotto-style for a creamy alternative to rice.

Hummus from the Pot

Makes 1 quart

In *Zahav: A World of Israeli Cooking,* we took the long road to our ideal hummus—it's what we serve at our restaurants. In *Israeli Soul,* we used canned chickpeas to power our 5-Minute Hummus. Now, the Instant Pot changes the game again, letting us quickly cook dried chickpeas with no presoaking or hours of boiling, and allowing us to use warm chickpeas—it's a whole other level of dreaminess.

- 1 recipe Instant Pot Chickpeas (recipe at right), still warm
- Scant 2 cups Basic Tehina Sauce (see METHOD, page 264)
- 1 teaspoon salt
- ½ teaspoon cumin
- Olive oil and pimentón, for topping

• With a slotted spoon, transfer the warm chickpeas to a food processor, reserving the cooking liquid, and add the Basic Tehina Sauce, salt, and cumin.

• Pulse to blend, gradually adding cooking liquid to loosen, as needed. The hummus will be ready when it's creamy and smooth.

• Serve topped with olive oil and pimentón.

Instant Pot Chickpeas

Makes 3 cups

- 1 cup dried chickpeas
- 8 cups water
- 1½ teaspoons salt

• Place the chickpeas, water, and salt in your multicooker.

• Program your multicooker to the pressure cooker setting according to the manufacturer's instructions. Make sure the steam release handle is sealed. Set the timer for 55 minutes.

• Turn on the "keep warm" function so the chickpeas will stay warm once cooked.

Basic Tehina Sauce

Makes 2 cups

This is one recipe that hasn't changed a bit since we started using it at Zahav fifteen years ago. It's a dip, a sauce, a salad dressing, and, of course, an indispensable component for making great hummus.

- 5 garlic cloves
- 5 tablespoons lemon juice (from 1½ lemons)
- ¾ teaspoon salt
- 1 cup tehina
- ¼ teaspoon ground cumin
- About ¾ cup very cold water

• In a food processor or high-powered blender, puree the garlic, lemon juice, and ½ teaspoon of the salt. Blend until you have a coarse puree. Let the mixture stand for 5 to 10 minutes to let the garlic mellow.

• Pour the mixture through a fine-meshed strainer set over a large mixing bowl, pressing on the solids to extract as much liquid as possible. Discard the solids.

• Stir in the tehina and the remaining ¼ teaspoon of salt.

• Whisk everything together until smooth, adding water a few tablespoons at a time. Continue adding water until you have a thick yet creamy sauce.

• Tehina will keep in the refrigerator for up to a week or frozen for up to a month.

Making: Hummus from the Pot

> "This method allows you to use chickpeas while they're still warm. Just like at an Israeli hummusiya." —*STEVE*

For ultra-creamy hummus, increase the cooking time on the chickpeas until they are beginning to lose their shape. And if you're pinched for time, canned chickpeas are a totally respectable substitute.

Masabacha

Makes 1 scant quart

Masabacha is a close cousin of hummus, where the cooked chickpeas are left whole or slightly crushed and dressed with tehina, lemon, and plenty of olive oil. It may look a bit messy, but it's a totally luxurious dish, especially when the chickpeas are still warm. The tehina will seize up when it comes into contact with the chickpeas, so don't be afraid to use the cooking liquid to thin it out and keep everything swimming and dreamy.

We garnish with tons of parsley and some chopped shipka peppers for their acidic kick. And if you really want to eat it the Israeli way, scoop the masabacha up with a petal of raw onion.

> "'Masabacha' in Arabic means 'swimming'—just what whole chickpeas do in their tehina sauce." —*STEVE*

- 1 recipe Instant Pot Chickpeas (see page 262)
- ½ cup Basic Tehina Sauce (see METHOD, page 264)
- Juice of ½ lemon
- 1 shipka pepper, finely chopped
- ¼ cup finely chopped parsley, plus more for topping
- 1 teaspoon salt
- Olive oil, for drizzling
- Onion petals, for scooping
- Lemon wedges, for serving

• With a slotted spoon, transfer the warm chickpeas to a large bowl, reserving the cooking liquid. With a fork, lightly mash some of the chickpeas.

• Stir in the Basic Tehina Sauce and the lemon juice, and gradually add cooking liquid to loosen the sauce, as needed. Stir in the chopped shipka pepper, parsley, and salt.

• Finish with a generous drizzling of olive oil and a sprinkle of chopped parsley.

• Serve with onion petals for scooping and lemon wedges.

"These recipes are our love letter to freekah." —*MIKE*

Freekah Mujadara

Makes 6 hearty servings

Although rice is the better-known mujadara base, in the Galilee and elsewhere in the Levant, freekah is a traditional variant. Freekah refers specifically to green wheat that's processed by burning away the straw and chaff, leaving only the seeds behind, giving freekah its beguiling signature smoky flavor. "Mujadara" means "pockmarked," a rather inelegant term that refers to the texture of the lentils and grains.

Three distinctly flavored elements come together to make this classic, super-nutritious regional staple: caramelized onions, cinnamon-scented lentils, and steamed freekah. Make sure to give the freekah a good rinse before cooking.

FOR THE FREEKAH

- 1 cup freekah, rinsed
- 1 teaspoon salt
- 2½ cups water

• In a medium pot, add the freekah, salt, and water. Cover and bring to a boil over medium-high heat. (Watch for the steam; that's your cue that the water is boiling.)

• Reduce the heat to medium-low and cook until tender, about 20 minutes.

• Keep covered, off the heat. Place a dish towel under the lid to help absorb moisture from the freekah during its rest.

• When ready to assemble the mujadara, fluff the freekah with a fork. Drain off any residual water.

FOR THE LENTILS

- 1 cup beluga lentils
- ½ teaspoon salt
- ¼ medium onion, peeled and left whole
- 1 cinnamon stick
- 3 cups water

• In a medium saucepan set over medium heat, add the lentils, salt, onion, cinnamon stick, and water. Bring to a boil, then cover and reduce the heat to medium-low.

• Cook until the lentils are tender, 25 to 30 minutes, then drain.

FOR ASSEMBLY

- 1 recipe Caramelized Onions (see METHOD, page 38)
- ½ to 1 teaspoon salt, for seasoning

• In a medium bowl, add the caramelized onions, freekah, and lentils, and gently toss until evenly coated. Season with the salt, as needed.

Mujadara with Slow-Roasted Salmon

Makes 4 servings

Salmon gets a bad rap for being overused. But there are good reasons: It's high fat content makes it one of the simplest, most crowd-pleasing fish to cook. And it's easy to find affordable, sustainably raised salmon. Salmon with mujadara is our idea of a delicious pairing. A dollop of labneh and a sprinkling of sumac makes it a healthy, delicious, and easy weekday meal with sophisticated weekend vibes.

2 to 4 salmon fillets
Salt, for seasoning
Ground sumac, for seasoning
Freekah Mujadara (page 269)
Labneh, for serving
Olive oil, for finishing

- Preheat the oven to 300° F. Arrange the salmon in a single layer on a sheet pan and season with salt on both sides.
- Generously sprinkle sumac on top, about ½ teaspoon per fillet.
- Cook until the salmon is opaque and easily flakes with a fork, about 15 minutes.
- To serve, spoon mujadara into bowls, add the salmon, and top with 1 tablespoon of labneh, a drizzle of olive oil, and a pinch of sumac.

“If asparagus is not in season, use frozen peas. Or kale.” —MIKE

Freekah with Chicken, Almonds & Asparagus

Makes 4 hearty servings

This soul-satisfying, one-pot meal—a beautiful marriage of simple ingredients—is lifted by the incomparable notes of baharat (Mike calls it Middle Eastern pumpkin pie spice!).

- 4 bone-in, skin-on chicken thighs, trimmed as needed
- 1 tablespoon plus ½ teaspoon baharat
- 2 teaspoons salt, plus more for seasoning the chicken
- ¼ cup olive oil, plus 1 tablespoon for toasting
- ½ large onion, finely chopped
- 1 cup freekah, rinsed
- 1 bunch asparagus, chopped
- ¾ cup sliced almonds
- Lemon wedges, for serving

• Coat both sides of the chicken with 1 tablespoon of the baharat. Season liberally with salt on both sides.

• Pour the ¼ cup of olive oil into a large skillet set over medium-high heat. Lay the chicken thighs, skin side down, into the pan.

• Cook the first side until the skin is golden brown, about 8 minutes.

• Turn with tongs and cook until the juices run clear, about 20 minutes. Adjust the heat as needed to avoid burning the browned bits on the bottom of the pan.

• Transfer the chicken to a plate.

• Reduce the heat to medium and add the onion to the skillet, stirring to coat with the rendered fat. Add a few tablespoons of water to help loosen the stuck-on bits.

• Stir in the freekah, 1 teaspoon of the salt, and the remaining ½ teaspoon of baharat.

• Have about 4 cups of water on hand. Add ½ cup of water and bring to a simmer. Stir frequently until the water is nearly absorbed. Continue to add water in ½-cup increments until the freekah is tender, about 20 minutes.

• Drain any residual chicken juices from the plate back into the pan. Cover the pan and keep on low heat.

• When the chicken is cool to the touch, remove the skins and reserve. Cut the meat off the bones and chop into 1-inch pieces.

• Add the chopped asparagus (or peas or kale) to the pan, stirring until evenly mixed. Stir in the chicken. Cover and cook over low heat to let the vegetables steam, about 5 minutes.

• Meanwhile, toast the almonds with the 1 tablespoon of olive oil in a small skillet. We like to stir the chicken skins, finely chopped, into the toasted nuts in the pan.

• Taste the freekah-chicken mixture for salt before serving and add up to 1 teaspoon as needed.

• Spoon into bowls and scatter the almond mixture on top. Serve with lemon wedges.

Making: Freekah with Chicken, Almonds & Asparagus

The fond that sticks to the bottom of the pan while the chicken is browning will dissolve with the freekah cooking liquid and add tons of flavor. Manage the heat to prevent the fond from getting too dark and adding a burnt note to the finished dish.

> "Gotta take our time with the chicken thighs to keep the tasty bits from burning." —*MIKE*

"We cook the freekah in the same pan to take advantage of all that good chicken flavor." —*STEVE*

The freekah is cooked risotto-style—by adding small amounts of liquid and letting it almost fully absorb before adding more. Time the addition of the asparagus and chicken so that they are warmed through by the time the freekah is cooked.

Freekah Tabbouleh with Kale

Makes 4 or 5 servings

This is a robust turn on the traditional parsley-and-bulgur-based salad, made even more luscious with the addition of sweet summer corn. The food processor makes quick work of the kale chopping.

"Kale instead of parsley—freekah instead of bulgur." —*MIKE*

- 2 medium ears corn, husks on
- 1 cup freekah, rinsed
- 2 teaspoons salt
- 2½ cups water
- 1 bunch kale
- 3 Persian cucumbers, cut into 1-inch pieces
- 1 pint cherry tomatoes, halved or quartered
- Juice of 1½ lemons
- Olive oil, for drizzling

• Roast the corn: Preheat the oven to 400°F. Place the corn on a sheet pan and roast for about 30 minutes.

• Let the ears of corn cool before removing the husks. Cut the kernels off the cob.

• Meanwhile, cook the freekah: Place the freekah in a medium saucepan. Add 1 teaspoon of the salt and the water. Cover and bring to a boil over high heat. Reduce the heat to medium-low and cook until tender, about 20 minutes. Let the freekah rest, covered, for at least 10 minutes. Cool, and drain if needed.

• Put the kale in a food processor and process until it's very finely chopped and resembles minced parsley. Transfer the kale to a large bowl.

• Scatter the corn kernels on top of the kale.

• Add the cucumbers to the bowl, follow with the tomatoes, then add the cooked freekah.

• Stir until evenly mixed. Season with the remaining 1 teaspoon of salt and the lemon juice, stirring until evenly coated. Drizzle with olive oil before serving.

Israeli Couscous & Meatballs

Makes about 75 small meatballs

"P'titim" is the Hebrew word for Israeli couscous, those tiny balls of toasted pasta developed by the Osem company in the 1950s in response to a relative shortage of rice and relative surplus of wheat. We love it for its quick cooking time and its appeal to children. For extra flavor, we cook the p'titim directly in the sauce.

FOR THE MEATBALLS

- 1 pound ground beef
- 2 large eggs, lightly beaten
- ½ large onion, grated or very finely chopped
- ½ cup plain breadcrumbs
- 2 tablespoons za'atar
- 1 teaspoon salt
- ½ cup grated Parmigiano-Reggiano cheese, plus more for topping
- Olive oil, for drizzling

FOR THE SAUCE

- 1 cup Israeli couscous
- ¼ cup olive oil
- 6 garlic cloves, thinly sliced
- 1 2-by-1-inch piece fresh ginger, peeled and very finely chopped
- 1 28-ounce can crushed tomatoes
- 2 teaspoons North African Spice Blend (see METHOD, page 281)
- 2 teaspoons sugar
- 2 cups water

• In a large bowl, combine the meat, eggs, onion, breadcrumbs, za'atar, and salt, stirring or mixing by hand. Add the cheese, stirring until evenly mixed.

• Set the oven to the high broiler setting.

• Form the seasoned meat into small balls, about ½ inch in diameter.

• Arrange the meatballs in a single layer on a sheet pan and drizzle olive oil on top.

• Broil until browned, about 5 minutes.

• Preheat the oven to 400°F. Place the couscous on a sheet pan and toast until golden, about 7 minutes.

• Pour the oil into a large skillet set over medium heat. Stir in the garlic and ginger, cooking until aromatic, about 2 minutes. Add the tomatoes and their juices, spice blend, and sugar, stirring until evenly mixed. Add the water and bring the mixture to a rapid boil.

• Stir in the couscous and cover, cooking until tender, 10 minutes.

• Transfer the meatballs to the sauce and warm for 5 minutes. Sprinkle grated cheese on top.

POWDER
MOUNTAIN

METHOD

North African Spice Blend

Makes about ¼ cup

We love the edge this signature spice blend gives to tomato sauce, but it's also great as a rub on poultry, a seasoning for roasted vegetables, and even as a flavor base for chili.

- 1 tablespoon coriander seeds
- 1 tablespoon cumin seeds
- 1 tablespoon caraway seeds
- ½ cinnamon stick
- Pinch salt

- Grind the spices and salt with a mortar and pestle, or in an electric spice grinder, until powdery.
- Store any extra spice blend in a small jar in a cool, dark place.

"It's therapeutic to bash whole spices with a heavy piece of granite!" —*STEVE*

Eggplant T'bit

Makes 6 servings

Here's a vegan version of the Iraqi celebratory dish traditionally eaten for lunch on Shabbat. The amba, tomato paste, cinnamon, and turmeric are rich in flavor. If the thought of unmolding this dish before your family and friends is terrifying, fear not: Even our perfect-looking t'bit was patched with pieces of eggplant that had stuck to the bottom of the pot.

- 2¾ teaspoons salt, plus more for the eggplant
- 1 medium eggplant, peeled, cut into ½-inch rounds
- 1 cup jasmine or basmati rice
- 2 tablespoons olive oil, plus more for brushing
- 1 head garlic, cloves separated and peeled
- 2 large carrots, cut into rounds
- ½ head cauliflower, florets separated
- 1 cinnamon stick
- 1¾ cups hot water
- 2 teaspoons tomato paste
- 1 teaspoon amba
- 1 teaspoon ground turmeric

• Generously salt the eggplant slices on top and let sit for about 30 minutes.

• Meanwhile, soak the rice for 30 minutes. Drain and place in a large bowl.

• Rinse the eggplant well. Squeeze by hand to remove as much water as possible.

• Arrange the eggplant slices in a single layer on a sheet pan and brush the tops with olive oil. Set the oven to the low broiler setting. Cook until the eggplant is tender and reaches a deeply roasted color, 30 to 35 minutes. (If you have made the Sabich on page 175, this process will be familiar.)

• In another bowl, stir together the garlic, carrots, cauliflower, 2 teaspoons of the salt, and the 2 tablespoons of olive oil.

• Transfer to a sheet pan and arrange in a single layer. Broil until tender and golden, about 20 minutes. Transfer to the bowl containing the drained rice, stirring together until evenly mixed.

• Using olive oil, generously coat the sides and bottom of a medium (3- to 4-quart) enameled cast-iron pot. Line the bottom with the broiled eggplant and cover the sides as much as possible.

• Spoon the vegetable-rice mixture on top of the eggplant, pressing it down to compress. Tuck the cinnamon stick into the rice like a buried treasure.

• In another bowl, whisk together the hot water, tomato paste, amba, turmeric, and the remaining ¾ teaspoon of salt.

• Pour the spiced liquid on top of the rice. Cover and place the pot over medium-high heat. Bring to a boil, then reduce the heat to low. Cook for 25 minutes.

• Remove the pot from the heat and let the t'bit rest, covered, for an hour.

• Carefully(!) invert onto a large platter.

Making: Eggplant T'bit

Oil the bottom and sides of the pot really well to avoid sticking. And layer the eggplant on the bottom of the pot as snugly as possible to prevent it from floating up during cooking.

"Besides the fact that there's actually no meat in it, you'd never be able to tell that this t'bit is vegan." —*STEVE*

Beef Hamin

Makes 6 servings

"Hamin" means "warm" in Hebrew and refers to a family of Sephardic meat stews slowly cooked overnight and served hot for Shabbat lunch. During the Inquisition, hamin on the table was incriminating evidence of Jews maintaining their religious practice. Over time, the tradition spread across the Jewish world—in Europe it became "cholent"; in North Africa it became "dafina"; in Iraq it became "t'bit" (see page 282). We use dried fruit, cinnamon, and a healthy dose of harissa to give it a Moroccan-Israeli pedigree.

The wheat berries are perfect here, since they retain their shape over the long cooking. But: Do plan in advance, since both the wheat berries and the chickpeas need to soak overnight before cooking.

- 3 large Yukon potatoes, quartered
- 3 tablespoons olive oil
- 3½ teaspoons salt
- 1½ pounds beef chuck, cubed
- ½ cup plus 1 heaping teaspoon harissa
- 1 heaping tablespoon tomato paste
- 4 cups hot water
- 1 cup dried chickpeas, soaked overnight and drained
- ½ cup wheat berries, soaked overnight and drained
- 8 pitted dates
- 12 dried apricots
- 1 large onion, cut into wedges, with root intact
- Small handful of cilantro for the pot, plus fresh cilantro leaves for finishing
- 2 cinnamon sticks

• Set the oven to the high broiler setting.

• In a medium bowl, stir together the potatoes, 2 tablespoons of the olive oil, and ½ teaspoon of the salt. Arrange cut side up on a sheet pan. Place under the broiler and cook until golden, 12 to 15 minutes.

• In another medium bowl, season the meat with 1 teaspoon of the salt, the remaining 1 tablespoon of olive oil, and the 1 heaping teaspoon of harissa, turning until evenly coated.

• Place on a sheet pan under the broiler and cook until the top is well-seared, 8 to 10 minutes.

• In a third bowl, stir together the tomato paste and 1 cup of the hot water until the tomato paste is dissolved. Transfer to a stew pot.

• Preheat the oven to 250°F. Add the soaked chickpeas and wheat berries, dates, apricots, onion, cilantro, and cinnamon sticks to the pot. Add the ½ cup of harissa, the remaining 2 teaspoons of salt, the tomato paste mixture, and the remaining 3 cups of hot water. Finally, add the meat and its juices, plus the potatoes.

• Cover and place in the oven. Cook until the meat is extremely tender, about 4 hours. Serve in bowls with fresh cilantro.

"Adding dried fruit to slow-cooked savory dishes makes the magic happen." —*MIKE*

Making: Beef Hamin

"There is nothing better on a Shabbat afternoon than a bowl of stick-to-your-ribs hamin . . . followed immediately by a nap." —*STEVE*

Broiling the meat in advance is a great way to achieve browning without the mess of searing it in a pan. Broiling the potatoes before adding them to the pot forms a golden skin that helps them retain their structure during the long braise.

Chicken Maqluba

Makes 5 or 6 servings

The number of classic dishes in world cuisine that bring together chicken and rice are legion—think arroz con pollo, biryani, jollof, and paella. But few are as dramatic and delicious as the Palestinian maqluba, which means "upside down" in Arabic. The dish is built in its cooking pot from the bottom up. The magic comes with inverting the pot onto a platter for serving. It's a real showstopper!

- 1 cup basmati rice
- 1 teaspoon ground coriander
- 1 teaspoon ground cumin
- 1 teaspoon ground caraway
- 1 small whole chicken, 2 to 3 pounds, backbone removed (see page 120)
- 1½ teaspoons salt, plus more for seasoning
- ¼ cup olive oil
- 1 large red onion
- 2 teaspoons ground sumac
- 1 tablespoon red wine vinegar
- ¾ cup unsalted peanuts, pistachios, or almonds, toasted
- ¼ cup chopped parsley
- 5 cardamom pods
- 1 cup water
- Lemon wedges, for serving

• Soak the rice for 30 minutes. Drain and set aside.

• In a small bowl, stir together the coriander, cumin, and caraway.

• Rub the spice blend all over the skin side of the chicken. Liberally season with salt, between 1 and 2 teaspoons, depending on size of the chicken.

• Pour the oil into a large enameled cast-iron pot set over medium-high heat.

• Lay the chicken skin side down to sear. Reduce the heat to medium and cook, uncovered, for 10 minutes.

• Cut half of the onion into wedges. Transfer the wedges to the pot, tucking them alongside the chicken. Cover and cook for 10 minutes.

• Slice the remaining half of the onion into thin half-moons. Place in a small bowl and stir in the sumac, vinegar, and a few pinches of salt. Let the sumac onion marinate while you cook.

• Add the rice, nuts, parsley, and cardamom to the pot with the chicken.

• In a small bowl, stir together the water and the 1½ teaspoons of salt until the salt dissolves. Pour into the pot. Cover and cook for 20 minutes over medium-low heat.

• Off the heat, keep the pot covered for about 1 hour. Carefully invert onto a platter.

• Serve with the sumac onion and lemon wedges.

Making: Chicken Maqluba

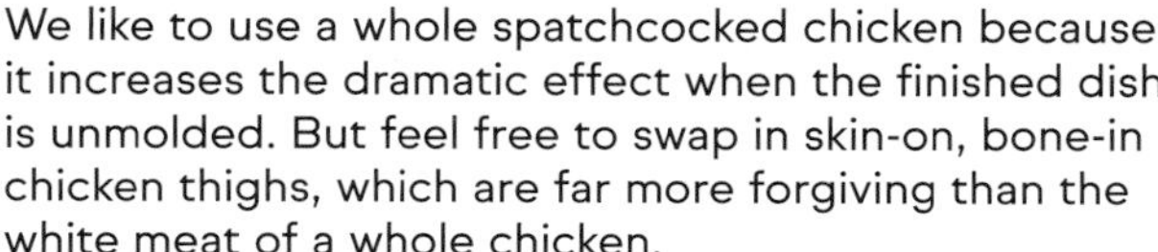

We like to use a whole spatchcocked chicken because it increases the dramatic effect when the finished dish is unmolded. But feel free to swap in skin-on, bone-in chicken thighs, which are far more forgiving than the white meat of a whole chicken.

"The chicken flavors the rice, and the rice insulates the chicken and keeps it moist. It's a virtuous circle!"—*MIKE*

7.

"Sustainably raised salmon from responsible fisheries (that's key!) makes this luxury fish more accessible and affordable." —*STEVE*

Fish

Date-Glazed Salmon Fillets

Makes 4 servings

The broiler is a great stand-in for the grill. Take care to manage the distance between the oven rack and the broiler element to prevent burning the skin. And look for date molasses with no sugar added; its flavor is more complex.

"There's always someone at the table who won't eat grilled salmon skin, so . . . more for me." —*STEVE*

Neutral oil, for the grill rack
4 6- to 8-ounce skin-on salmon fillets or a 1½-pound center-cut fillet, cut into pieces
2 teaspoons salt
2 teaspoons ground Urfa pepper
¼ cup date molasses

- Lightly oil a grill grate (or a cooling rack, if you're broiling).
- Season each fillet on both sides with about ½ teaspoon salt.
- Sprinkle the Urfa pepper on the flesh side until well-coated, about ½ teaspoon per fillet.
- Preheat the grill or set the oven to the low broiler setting.
- Cook the salmon skin side down (in the broiler, skin side up) for 3 to 5 minutes.
- Turn the fillets and brush date molasses on the side that's now on top.
- Cook for 3 to 5 minutes.
- Turn the fillets again and press on the fish with a metal spatula. Brush date molasses on the second side, and cook for 1 more minute.

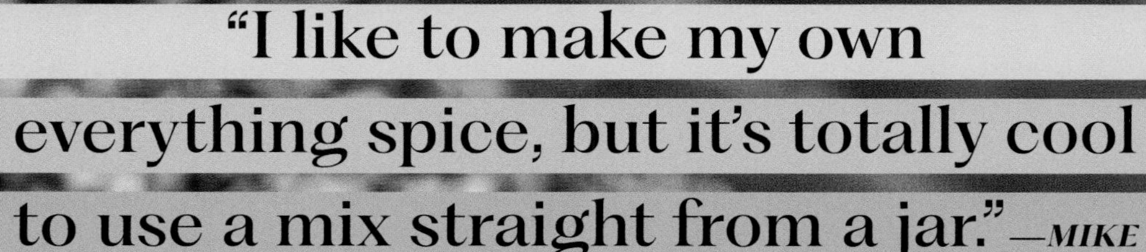
"I like to make my own
everything spice, but it's totally cool
to use a mix straight from a jar." —MIKE

Everything-Spiced Salmon
with Labneh Mashed Potatoes

Makes 4 or 5 servings

This is a spectacular-looking salmon preparation that's a major crowd-pleaser and takes less than five minutes to throw together. Beyond bagels, we believe almost *anything* can be improved by adding everything spice: eggs, pasta, avocados . . . even ice cream.

FOR THE POTATOES

- 6 medium Yukon potatoes, skin on
- 3 tablespoons salt, plus more for seasoning
- 1 cup labneh
- 2 tablespoons stemmed and finely chopped dill
- 2 tablespoons chopped scallions or chives, for finishing

• In a large pot, cover the potatoes with cold water, plus an inch or two above. Add the salt; the water should be good and salty to flavor the potatoes.

• Bring to a rapid boil over high heat, then reduce the heat to medium. Cook until the potatoes are paring-knife tender, about 25 minutes.

• Drain and transfer to a bowl. When the potatoes are just cool enough to handle, peel them into a large bowl. Mash them by hand with a big spoon or potato masher. Stir in the labneh, then the dill, until well-mixed. Taste for salt and add more as needed.

• Sprinkle the scallions on top and serve hot with the salmon.

• Mashed potatoes reheat well in a microwave. Cover with plastic wrap and reheat until warmed through.

FOR THE FISH

- 2 pounds center-cut salmon, ideally wild
- 2 tablespoons Dijon mustard
- 2 to 4 tablespoons everything spice, homemade (see recipe below) or store-bought

EVERYTHING SPICE

Stir together ½ cup toasted sesame seeds (half black, half white, for look!); ½ cup poppy seeds; ¼ cup minced dehydrated garlic; ¼ cup minced dehydrated onion; and ¼ cup coarse salt. Store in an airtight jar.

• Preheat the oven to 400°F.

• With a paper towel, pat the fish dry on both sides. Place skin side down on a sheet pan or in a baking dish.

• With a table knife or brush, paint the mustard all over the salmon.

• Sprinkle the everything spice on top of the mustard until the salmon is completely covered.

• Bake until the salmon's flesh is opaque and flakes easily with a fork—12 to 15 minutes.

• Serve with the mashed potatoes.

Making: Everything-Spiced Salmon with Labneh Mashed Potatoes

Don't skimp on the mustard. It helps the spice adhere to and fully coat the fish, and it tastes pretty good, too! We make our own everything spice, but it's totally fine to use it straight from a jar.

"The secret to good mashed potatoes: Boil them with their skins on, peel them while they're still hot, then mash immediately." —*STEVE*

Grilled Tuna
with Harissa & Tehina

Makes 4 servings

This is a super-robust fish dish that will even please meat-a-tarians. Make sure your grill is ripping hot so the tuna can get a nice char without overcooking. We like to serve tuna medium rare; for medium, grill for an extra minute per side. For well-done, save your money and just open a can.

- 2 1-inch-thick tuna steaks
- 2½ teaspoons Three C's Spice Blend (stir together 1 teaspoon each ground coriander and ground cumin, ½ teaspoon ground caraway, and a pinch or two ground cardamom)
- Salt, for seasoning
- 2 tablespoons harissa, plus more for finishing
- 1 to 2 teaspoons olive oil
- 1 cup Basic Tehina Sauce (see METHOD, page 264)
- Lemon wedges, for serving

- With a paper towel, pat both sides of the fish dry.
- Generously season both sides with the Three C's Spice Blend and salt.
- In a small bowl, mix the harissa with the olive oil, enough to loosen the harissa, with a fork.
- Preheat the grill until it's very hot or set the oven to the high broiler setting.
- Lightly oil a grill grate (or a cooling rack, if you're broiling).
- Cook the tuna on the first side for 2 minutes. Turn over. Brush the harissa on top. Cook for 2 minutes. When the sides of the fish turn beige, that's your doneness cue.
- Remove the tuna steaks from the heat and let rest for about 5 minutes.
- Slice the steaks crosswise.
- Drizzle with Basic Tehina Sauce and harissa.
- Serve with lemon wedges.

Grilled Trout with Chermoula

Makes 4 servings

We love cooking butterflied trout over coals. The fish is thin enough to cook almost entirely on the skin side, ensuring that it gets nice and crispy and has enough time over the heat to release without sticking (we recommend oiling the grill grates for extra insurance). A brief "kiss" on the flesh side will caramelize the chermoula paste—which works well as a rub or marinade for any number of grilled meats.

- 2 teaspoons coriander seeds
- 1 teaspoon caraway seeds
- 1 teaspoon dill seeds
- 1 teaspoon salt, plus more for seasoning
- 4 garlic cloves, minced
- 2 shallots, minced
- 1 2-inch piece ginger, peeled and minced
- 1 green chile pepper (jalapeño or serrano), seeded and very finely diced
- 2 tablespoons tomato paste
- ¼ cup olive oil
- Neutral oil, for the pan
- 2 1-pound rainbow trout, scaled, gutted, and butterflied

• For the chermoula, use a mortar and pestle to grind the coriander, caraway, and dill seeds with the salt until fine, and transfer to a bowl.

• Using a mortar and pestle or mini chopper, pulverize the garlic, shallots, ginger, and chile pepper until as smooth as possible. If it still feels chunky, grind it a bit more. Add to the bowl of spices.

• Add the tomato paste. Stir with the spices until evenly mixed. The chermoula should be thick and smooth.

• In a small skillet set over medium heat, warm the olive oil. Add the chermoula and heat until the sauce is aromatic and most of the oil is absorbed, about 3 minutes.

• Transfer to a plate and refrigerate to cool.

• Season both sides of each trout with salt. With a table knife, spread the chermoula paste on the flesh side of each trout.

• Lightly oil a grill grate (or cooling rack if using the broiler). Or set the broiler low and move an oven rack close to the heating element.

• Lay the fish skin side down (for broiler, skin side up). Cook until opaque and almost cooked through, 6 to 8 minutes. The chermoula will bubble slightly. Flip and cook the flesh side for 1 additional minute.

Making: Chermoula for Grilled Trout

"Andrew Henshaw makes a version of this North African spice paste for branzino at Laser Wolf." —*STEVE*

"Chermoula is an incredible rub for barbecued chicken as well."—*MIKE*

This chile and spice mixture borrows techniques from southeast Asian and Mexican cooking. First the aromatics and spices are pounded into submission (a food processor is an acceptable—if less authentic—mixing option). Then everything is fried in oil to deepen the flavors.

Fish Chraime

Makes 4 or 5 servings

Our French training taught us to treat fish like a delicate flower, so of course, we love the way chraime thumbs its nose at this orthodoxy in favor of a rich, fiery fish stew. The oil preserves the fish and keeps it moist. In North Africa, chraime was traditionally cooked on Friday before Shabbat and served at room temp the next day. We love to finish the dish with a handful of fried shallots, some seared shishito peppers, and lots of cilantro. For another version of chraime, see Cauliflower Chraime, page 182.

- 1 cup olive oil
- 1 large onion, diced
- 6 to 8 garlic cloves, depending on size, thinly sliced
- 1 red bell pepper, diced
- ¼ cup harissa
- Scant 1 cup crushed tomatoes (from a 15-ounce can)
- ½ cup stemmed and roughly chopped cilantro
- Salt, for seasoning
- 1½ pounds grouper, skin removed, cut into 2-ounce pieces
- 12 shishito peppers
- ½ lemon, for finishing
- Fried shallots, for finishing

• In a large skillet set over medium-low heat, add the oil and onion. When the onion begins to soften, add the garlic, then the bell pepper. Cook for about 30 minutes.

• Harissa goes in next to coat the vegetables and bloom in the oil, followed by the tomatoes and their juices and half of the cilantro. Stir until evenly mixed. The sauce will be aromatic and gutsy.

• Sprinkle salt over the fish, then lay the fish into the sauce, turning the pieces until evenly coated.

• Cover and continue cooking over medium-low heat until the fish is opaque, 5 minutes or more.

• In another large skillet, quickly pan-sear the shishito peppers until softened.

• Remove the chraime from the heat, add the seared peppers and the remaining cilantro, and squeeze some lemon juice on top. Then sprinkle on the fried shallots.

• Serve hot or at room temperature.

"We've come to use 'chraime' as a verb, as in 'Let's *chraime* that cauliflower!'" —*MIKE*

Cod in Grape Leaves
with Labneh Tzatziki & Grapes

Makes 4 servings

Briny grape leaves lightly cure the fish and keep it moist. We serve these little bundles with a cooling tzatziki, a Middle Eastern yogurt and herb sauce, enhanced with chopped green grapes, which add a burst of sweetness to counter the yogurt's acidity.

FOR THE TZATZIKI

- 1 pint labneh
- 2 Persian cucumbers, finely chopped
- 1 cup seedless green grapes, quartered
- 2 shallots, finely chopped
- 1 tablespoon finely chopped mint leaves
- ½ cup stemmed and finely chopped dill
- 1 garlic clove, finely grated
- 2 to 4 tablespoons fresh lemon juice
- Salt, for seasoning

• Put the labneh into a medium bowl. Add the cucumbers, grapes, shallots, mint, dill, and garlic. Stir until evenly mixed.

• Gradually add the lemon juice, tasting and adding more as needed.

• Add salt to taste.

FOR THE FISH

- 1½ pounds wild cod
- Salt, for seasoning
- About 1 tablespoon olive oil, plus more for finishing
- 8 to 12 grape leaves
- 1 lemon, quartered, for serving

• Preheat the oven to 400°F. Cut the fish into 4 equal pieces, 5 to 6 ounces each. Pat each piece dry with a paper towel. Season both sides with salt.

• Drizzle the olive oil onto a sheet pan. Arrange 4 of the grape leaves on the pan, a few inches apart. Think of these as lily pads for each piece of fish.

• Wrap each piece of fish in the remaining grape leaves, using two if needed. It's okay if there are a few little holes.

• Place each grape leaf parcel on top of a lily pad.

• Bake for 10 minutes. Then set the oven to low broil, allowing the grape leaves to crisp up a bit, 1 to 2 minutes.

• Spoon some tzatziki onto plates and top each with a packet of grape-leaf-wrapped cod.

• Drizzle with olive oil and serve with the lemon quarters.

Making: Cod in Grape Leaves with Labneh Tzatziki & Grapes

Don't worry if the packages don't resemble perfect gift-wrapped presents; it's more important to avoid too much overlapping of grape leaves, which makes them unpleasantly chewy after cooking.

"The grape leaves both season and insulate the fish. And they get nicely crispy in the oven."—*STEVE*

> "I love the magic of a simple brined grape leaf from a jar flavoring the cod!" —*MIKE*

We believe you can never put too many herbs in tzatziki, so don't get hung up on exact measurements. Tzatziki is a versatile and delicious dip on its own, with or without the grapes. May we suggest some thick-cut potato chips?

Kataifi-Wrapped Halibut

Makes 4 servings

Kataifi, the threadlike shredded cousin of phyllo dough, makes an ideal fish wrapper: It gets super crunchy in the oven (butter helps!) and insulates the delicate fish during cooking. This dish looks fancy enough for a dinner party, and once the fillets are wrapped, the oven does the work. We serve the fish with a quick Euro-inspired sauce of butter, lemon, capers, and almonds.

- 4 5- to 6-ounce halibut fillets, skin removed
- Salt, for seasoning
- ½ 16-ounce box kataifi, thawed
- 3 tablespoons olive oil
- ½ cup (1 stick) unsalted butter
- ½ cup sliced almonds
- 1 tablespoon capers, rinsed
- ½ preserved lemon, rinsed, seeded, and finely chopped
- ½ bunch parsley, stemmed and finely chopped
- Lemon wedges, for serving

• Preheat the oven to 400°F.

• With a paper towel, pat each fish fillet dry on both sides. Season both sides with salt.

• Cut the kataifi into four pieces with kitchen shears, making sure that each length is slightly larger than the fish on all sides.

• Lay a piece of fish on top of one piece of kataifi at the short end closest to you and roll up. Repeat with the other three pieces.

• Lightly drizzle olive oil in a 10-inch oven-friendly skillet. Lay the kataifi bundles in the pan, seam side down.

• Place 1 tablespoon of the butter on top of each bundle. Bake, uncovered, for 20 minutes.

• Set the oven to low broil and slide the fish under the heat until the kataifi tops are deeply brown, 1 to 2 minutes.

• Transfer the fish from the pan to the serving platter.

• Make the sauce: Over medium heat, melt the remaining 4 tablespoons of butter in the pan, stirring.

• Add the almonds, stirring until evenly coated. Watch for the butter beginning to foam. Remove from the heat when the foam begins to subside.

• Stir in the capers, preserved lemon, and parsley. Spoon pan sauce over the fish and serve with lemon wedges.

"Rolling these is all about the fingertips!" —MIKE

Making: Kataifi-Wrapped Halibut

Removing the skin from a fillet of fish takes some practice. (You can always ask your fishmonger to do it for you!) Another approach is to slice the fish into portions before removing the skin so you're working with smaller, more manageable pieces. Rolling the fish in kataifi is a snap. (For more on kataifi, see Chocolate Nut Kataifi "Purses," page 344.)

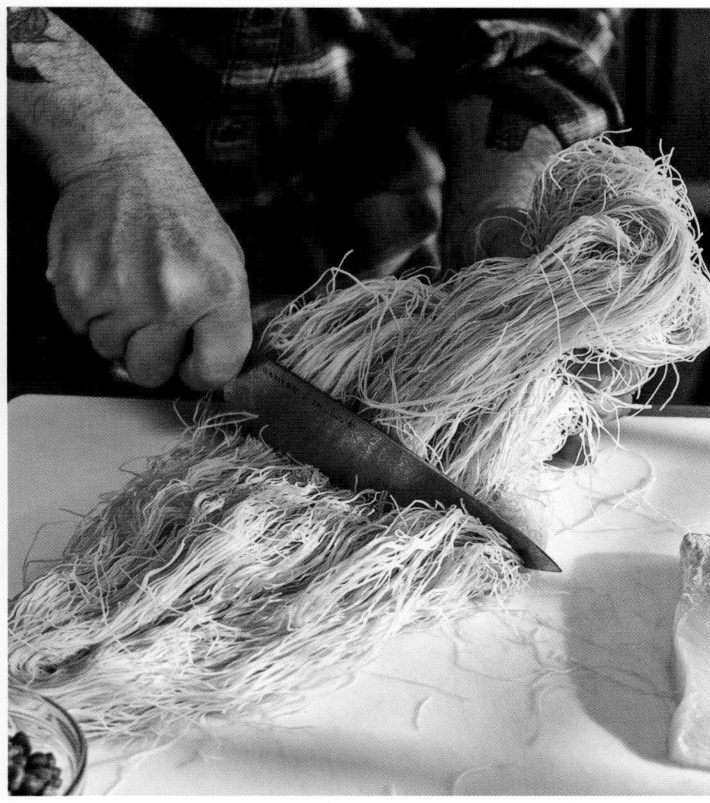

8.

“We think of sugar as a salt, used to bring out the flavor of other ingredients, not to overwhelm them.” —*MIKE*

Desserts

py
ml
225
175
125
75

Easy Honey-Tehina Slice & Bake Cookies

Makes 2 dozen

The nice thing about this cookie dough is that you can keep a log in the freezer and pull it out whenever the mood for fresh-baked cookies strikes you (or your children). We like to slightly *underbake* them so they stay a bit soft when cooled; the baking time depends on your oven.

- 1¼ cups all-purpose flour
- ¾ teaspoon baking powder
- ¼ teaspoon salt
- ½ cup (1 stick) butter, at room temperature, cut into tablespoon-size pieces
- ¼ cup brown sugar
- 2 tablespoons granulated sugar
- 3 tablespoons honey
- 3 tablespoons tehina

• In a medium bowl, stir together the flour, baking powder, and salt.

• In a stand mixer fitted with a paddle attachment (or in a large bowl with a handheld mixer), cream the butter and sugars until the mixture is smooth and light in color.

• Add the honey and tehina, mixing until blended. Stop and scrape the sides of the bowl as needed.

• With the mixer on low speed, add the flour mixture all at once, mixing until just combined.

• Transfer the dough onto plastic wrap and roll into a log about 12 inches long. Twist tightly at both ends to form a log approximately 2 inches in diameter.

• Refrigerate until the dough is firm, about 2 hours (or freeze for up to 3 months).

• Preheat the oven to 350°F.

• Spray a sheet pan with oil, then line it with parchment paper.

• Slice the cookie dough log into disks about ½ inch thick. Arrange on the pan about 2 inches apart.

• Bake until the cookies are golden brown around the edges, 14 to 16 minutes.

• Cool completely on the pan.

Making: Easy Honey-Tehina Slice & Bake Cookies

“I love these tight little rolls of cookie dough. It’s homemade slice and bake.” *—MIKE*

Make sure the dough is very cold when you slice the cookies so they hold their nice, round shape in the oven and don’t spread too much.

Baby Apple Cakes

Makes 1 dozen

Sweet but not too sweet, these babies are chock-full of apples and perfect for afternoon tea or school lunch boxes. The oil in the batter keeps the cakes moist; cardamom adds a warm note. A handheld mixer works fine here.

> "This is what we make when the kids come home from school starving." —*MIKE*

- Cooking spray or oil, for the pan
- 2½ cups all-purpose flour
- 1½ teaspoons ground cardamom
- 1 teaspoon baking powder
- ½ teaspoon baking soda
- ¼ teaspoon salt
- 2 eggs
- 1¾ cups sugar
- 1 teaspoon vanilla extract
- 1 cup neutral oil
- 2 cups finely chopped apples, skin on (from about 2 apples)

- Preheat the oven to 350°F.
- Oil a 12-cup muffin pan.
- In a medium bowl, stir together the flour, cardamom, baking powder, baking soda, and salt.
- In a stand mixer fitted with a paddle attachment, mix the eggs and sugar at low speed until smooth and light in color. Add the vanilla and oil, mixing until creamy and viscous.
- On low speed, add the flour mixture all at once, mixing until the flour is no longer visible.
- Scrape the sides of the bowl with a spatula. Fold in the chopped apples until evenly mixed.
- Pile the batter into each muffin cup; it's okay to go up to the rim.
- Bake for 15 minutes, then rotate the pan, front to back. Continue baking until golden on top, 10 to 15 minutes more.
- Let cool for a few minutes, then run a knife along the edges and remove the cakes, one at a time.
- The cakes keep well for 3 days in an airtight container, or in the freezer for up to 3 months.

Pistachio Sticky Buns

Makes 1 dozen

This is the most popular pastry we sell at K'far, Zahav's sister restaurant in Philadelphia and Brooklyn. "K'far" means "village" in Hebrew, and our "village" embraces both the town of K'far Saba in Israel, where Mike began to cook, as well as the Israeli restaurant village we've built in Philly. We use an Asian method called *tangzhong,* which involves first cooking a portion of the flour and liquid together, creating a fluffier dough that stays fresher longer. Making these buns is a two-day project.

FOR THE TANGZHONG

- 1 scant cup whole milk
- ⅓ cup bread flour

• Put the milk and flour into a small saucepan set over medium heat.

• Whisk constantly until the mixture thickens into a paste like brownie batter. Remove from the heat and let cool.

FOR THE DOUGH

- 1 cup whole milk, warmed to 100°F
- 1 tablespoon instant dry yeast
- 6 tablespoons sugar
- 3 eggs
- 6¼ cups bread flour, plus more for the work surface
- 2 teaspoons salt
- 10 tablespoons butter, at room temperature, cut into tablespoon-size pieces

• Pour the warm milk into a medium bowl. With a fork, whisk the yeast and 1 tablespoon of the sugar into the milk until nearly dissolved. Let sit for about 5 minutes; look for foam to form in the center of the mixture.

• Slowly pour the yeast mixture into the tangzhong (about a quarter at a time), using a whisk to blend. You'll end up with a thin paste.

• Whisk in the eggs, one at a time.

• Set up a stand mixer with a dough hook attachment. Add the flour and remaining 5 tablespoons of sugar to the bowl. Mix on the lowest setting and add the salt.

• Gradually pour the yeast and milk mixture on top of the flour and knead on low (speed 2 on a KitchenAid) for 5 minutes.

• Cover the dough with a kitchen towel and let it rest for 15 minutes.

• On medium speed, add the butter, one piece at a time. Incorporate each piece before adding more.

• Transfer the dough to an oiled bowl. Cover with plastic wrap for proofing.

• Now you have two options: Proof the dough either at room temperature in a non-drafty spot until doubled (about 2 hours), or overnight in the refrigerator.

• While the dough is proofing, make the caramel and filling.

(Continued on page 332)

Making: Tangzhong & Caramel for Pistachio Sticky Buns

Katreena Kanney is the executive pastry chef of K'Far, both for the restaurant itself as well as for our entire "village." Although she's somehow not a big fan of sweets, she's sure good at making them!

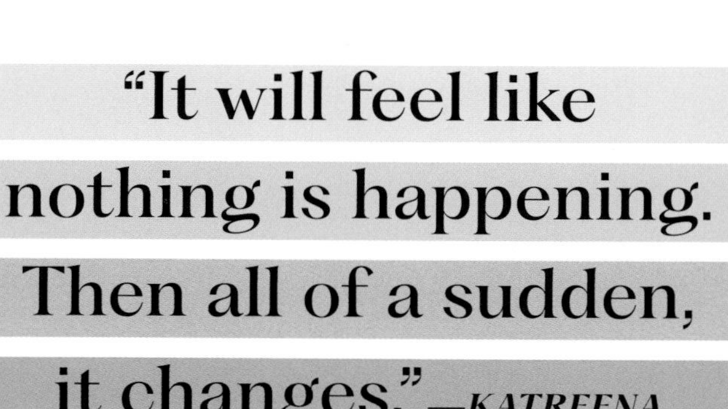

"It will feel like nothing is happening. Then all of a sudden, it changes." —*KATREENA*

Whisk the tangzhong the entire time you're cooking it or it will be lumpy. Once it's transformed into a thick, puddinglike paste, allow it to cool completely before incorporating it into the dough.

Technically we're making more of a butterscotch than a caramel, since we're not caramelizing the sugar but rather melting it with butter into a smooth sauce. It's important not to let the mixture get too hot, so the butter doesn't separate.

Making: Pistachio Sticky Buns

FOR THE CARAMEL

Neutral oil, for the pan
¾ cup (1½ sticks) butter
1½ cups brown sugar
2 tablespoons light corn syrup
2 teaspoons vanilla extract

• Before you make the caramel, oil and line a 13-by-9-inch rectangular pan with parchment paper. FYI: This is the pan in which you'll bake the buns.

• In a small saucepan set over low heat, melt the butter. As the butter melts, add the brown sugar, corn syrup, and vanilla, whisking until smooth.

• Two important notes: Do not let the mixture boil! And: Keep whisking! Your goal is to not let the butter and brown sugar separate.

• Pour the caramel into the prepared pan, making sure it completely covers the parchment.

FOR THE FILLING

1¾ cups whole unsalted shelled pistachios, plus ½ cup chopped for finishing
¼ cup granulated sugar
¼ cup brown sugar
¼ teaspoon salt
½ lemon, zested
½ cup (1 stick) butter, at room temperature, cut into tablespoon-size pieces

• In a food processor, blitz the whole pistachios, both sugars, salt, and lemon zest.

• You're making a thick paste with very finely ground pistachios, but leave some texture; this is not quite a nut butter.

• Gradually add the butter, mixing until it is no longer visible.

• Transfer the mixture to a bowl and keep at room temperature for easier spreading.

ROLLING & ASSEMBLY

- Lightly flour the work surface and roll the dough out into a rectangle approximately 12 inches wide by 18 inches long. The dough should be about ¼ inch thick.
- Spread the pistachio filling evenly on the dough from edge to edge.
- Roll the long edge of the dough closest to you into a log about 18 inches long.
- Cut the dough into 12 even pieces, each about 1½ inches wide.
- Carefully transfer the cut dough to the caramel-lined pan.
- Cover with a towel and let proof until the buns have doubled in size, 1 to 2 hours.
- When ready to bake, preheat the oven to 350°F.
- Bake until the buns are puffy and golden on top, 25 to 30 minutes.
- Let the buns rest 3 to 5 minutes to allow the caramel to cool and thicken.
- Carefully invert the pan onto a cutting board or serving dish.
- Top with the chopped pistachios and separate into buns.

"The pistachio filling acts as a glue and makes beautiful spirals." —*KATREENA*

Black Lime Bars
with White Chocolate Ganache

Makes 16

Here's a take on one of our all-time favorite desserts: Key lime pie. It's made almost entirely from pantry ingredients but depends on black limes—those small Persian limes that are sun-dried until they turn hard (and black). We like their complexity in sweets, and we've even dropped them whole or ground into savory soups and stews, too, where they add a sour, funky, smoky edge.

> **"I'll take a perfect balance of sweet and tart over chocolate any day."** —*STEVE*

FOR THE CRUST

- Neutral oil, for the parchment paper
- 1¼ cups graham cracker crumbs (from 9 to 10 graham crackers)
- ¼ cup almond flour
- 2 tablespoons brown sugar
- ¼ teaspoon salt
- ¼ teaspoon ground cinnamon
- 6 tablespoons (¾ stick) butter, melted

• Oil and line an 8-by-8-inch pan with parchment paper. Make sure there is a slight overhang to create a sling for removing the bars from the pan after baking.

• Preheat the oven to 350°F.

• In a medium bowl, stir together the graham cracker crumbs, almond flour, brown sugar, salt, and cinnamon.

• Stir in the melted butter.

• Press the mixture into the bottom of the prepared pan. Bake for 8 minutes. Cool slightly.

FOR THE FILLING

- 1 14-ounce can sweetened condensed milk
- 6 egg yolks
- 2 limes, zested
- 1 cup lime juice (from 8 limes)

• Reduce the oven temperature to 325°F.

• In a medium bowl, whisk together all the ingredients until completely blended.

• Pour into the slightly cooled crust.

• Bake until the filling has set but is still slightly jiggly in the middle, 20 to 25 minutes.

• Cool completely, then refrigerate until cold. Keep refrigerated until you're ready to make the ganache.

FOR THE WHITE CHOCOLATE GANACHE & ASSEMBLY

- ½ cup white chocolate chunks or chips
- ⅓ cup heavy cream
- 1½ teaspoons butter
- 1 teaspoon ground or grated black lime powder

• Chop the white chocolate and place the pieces in a small bowl.

• In a small saucepan, bring the cream just to a simmer, with teeny bubbles.

• Pour the cream over the white chocolate and whisk until smooth.

• Add the butter and black lime powder, whisking until the butter is no longer visible.

• To assemble the bars, pour the ganache over the lime filling and spread evenly.

• Return the bars to the refrigerator to firm up, about 1 hour.

• When ready to serve, grab the overhanging parchment to lift the bars out of the pan.

• With the parchment still lining the bottom, slice into 2-inch squares.

• To keep: Refrigerate in an airtight container.

Making: Black Lime Bars with White Chocolate Ganache

There are tools for separating eggs but none as cheap and effective as a clean pair of hands. Save the whites to make a pavlova (see page 352). A flat-bottomed cup is perfect for evenly tamping down the graham cracker crust.

> "I love to grate a little black lime into chicken soup." —*MIKE*

"I'm always tempted to skip this step; zesting limes by hand is a pain, but it really does make a difference." —*STEVE*

Both the filling and the crust can be made a day in advance, but the ganache spreads best when it's freshly made. White chocolate chips are readily available in supermarket baking aisles.

Sumac Lemonade

Makes 1 quart

Sumac is an important spice in Middle Eastern cooking, adding sourness without liquid, and bringing earthy and slightly salty flavors. Sumac is key in the spice blend za'atar and is celebrated in such Palestinian dishes as summaqiyya (a Gazan stew of lamb, tehina, and sumac). It's perfect in sweet things, too, like this gorgeous flame-colored lemonade. For a special treat, add a few drops of rose water.

- 1 cup sugar
- 1 cup water
- 2 tablespoons ground sumac
- ⅔ cup lemon juice (from 4 to 5 lemons)
- Cold still or sparkling water
- Fresh orange slices, optional

• In a small saucepan set over medium heat, stir together the sugar and water until the sugar is dissolved and the syrup has slightly thickened. Remove from the heat and stir in the sumac.

• Let the mixture steep for 1 hour.

• Strain and cool.

• When ready to serve, stir together the syrup and the lemon juice.

• Mix with cold still or sparkling water, using a one-to-one ratio. Add fresh orange slices if you like.

• You can make the syrup up to a week in advance, but for a real lemony pop, add the lemon juice just before serving.

"This just may be the original pink lemonade!" —MIKE

Pecan Cake

Makes 12 to 15 servings

With crispy edges and a tender interior, this pecan cake is a delicious showcase for a criminally overlooked nut. Did we mention it's gluten-free? A pecan flour batter is enriched with a homemade pecan butter and topped off with a cardamom-scented pecan crumble. You'll need a total of three scant cups of pecans. Toast them all at once, then measure what you need for each part of the recipe. (You can toast the nuts in a dry skillet, toaster oven, or in the oven at 250°F.) And this recipe will work with almost any nut!

FOR THE CRUMBLE

- 1½ cups pecans, lightly toasted
- ½ cup brown sugar
- 1 teaspoon ground cardamom
- 1 teaspoon ground cinnamon
- ½ teaspoon salt
- 2 tablespoons butter, melted

• Place everything but the butter in a food processor and blitz until the nuts are ground but still have a bit of texture. With the machine running, slowly stream in the butter, processing just until blended.

• Transfer to a small bowl.

FOR THE PECAN BUTTER

- ⅔ cup pecans, lightly toasted
- 2 tablespoons granulated sugar

• Using the same food processor bowl (no need to rinse), blitz the pecans and sugar. You're looking for the texture of peanut butter. Transfer to a small bowl.

FOR THE PECAN FLOUR & BATTER

- Cooking spray or oil, for the pan
- ¾ cup pecans, lightly toasted
- ⅓ cup cornstarch
- ⅔ cup almond flour
- 2 tablespoons rice flour
- ½ teaspoon salt
- ¼ teaspoon baking powder
- ¾ cup (1½ sticks) unsalted butter, at room temperature, cut into tablespoon-size pieces
- 1 cup granulated sugar
- 2 eggs
- 1 egg white
- 1 teaspoon vanilla extract
- Confectioners' sugar, for topping

• Use cooking spray to oil and parchment paper to line an 8- or 9-inch cake pan.

• Preheat the oven to 350°F.

• In the same food processor bowl (still no need to rinse), blitz the pecans and cornstarch until the nuts are finely ground. The texture should be sandy but not wet.

• Transfer this mixture to a medium bowl. Add the almond and rice flours, salt, and baking powder.

- Using a stand mixture with a paddle, cream the butter and granulated sugar together until smooth and light. Add the pecan butter, pulsing until evenly blended.
- Add the eggs, one at a time, followed by the egg white and vanilla extract.
- Add the dry ingredients all at once, mixing until just combined.
- With a spatula, turn the batter and look to make sure nothing has been left unmixed.
- Transfer the batter to the prepared pan.
- Top with the crumble, pressing down so that it adheres to the batter.
- Bake until a skewer inserted into the middle comes out clean, about 50 minutes.
- Cool the cake completely in the pan.
- Run a knife around the edge of the pan and turn the cake out onto a plate. Peel off the parchment and carefully invert the cake onto a plate or stand.
- Top with confectioners' sugar sifted through a strainer.

Making: Pecan Cake

A food processor can make the crumble, pecan butter, and pecan flour without having to be cleaned in between. It can handle the rest, too. But a stand mixer—for creaming the butter and sugar and for combining the batter without overmixing—is a more traditional (and more forgiving) tool.

Once the cake is out of the pan, the crumble layered on top will be on the bottom! So press a large serving plate on top and invert the cake once more so that the crumble is now on top, where it should be!

Chocolate Nut Kataifi "Purses"

Makes 1 dozen

There may be a million Middle Eastern pastries that combine kataifi with sugar and nuts and are drizzled with syrup, but perhaps none is as easy to make as these little "purses." Kataifi is a simple wheat dough that's extruded into threads. It's available frozen in the supermarket and looks like a skein of yarn when you open the package. Mixed with plenty of melted butter, the kataifi gets irresistibly crunchy in the oven.

FOR THE FILLING

- ½ cup dark or semisweet chocolate chips
- ¼ cup plus 2 tablespoons walnuts, toasted and roughly chopped
- ¼ cup plus 2 tablespoons pistachios, toasted and roughly chopped
- 2 tablespoons brown sugar
- ½ teaspoon ground cinnamon
- ¼ teaspoon salt

• In a medium bowl, stir together all the filling ingredients until evenly mixed. Set aside for assembly.

FOR THE SYRUP

- ½ cup water
- ½ cup granulated sugar
- 2 tablespoons honey

• In a small saucepan set over medium heat, stir together the water and sugar until the sugar is dissolved. Bring to a boil and add the honey. Cook until thickened, about 10 minutes, reducing the heat as needed.

FOR THE KATAIFI

- ½ 16-ounce box kataifi, thawed and roughly chopped
- ½ cup (1 stick) butter, melted (nondairy option: melted coconut oil)
- Cooking spray or oil, for the pan

• Pull apart the kataifi until it is free of clumps. Cut the kataifi threads across the grain to create short fibers.

• Pour the melted butter on top and turn the kataifi with your fingers until evenly coated and pliable.

• Use cooking spray to lightly oil a 12-cup muffin tin, and preheat the oven to 375°F.

• Press ¼ cup of the kataifi into each muffin cup. Press the kataifi up against the sides to mold into a cup shape. Spoon 1 tablespoon of the filling into each kataifi mold. Lay 1 tablespoon of the kataifi on top and press down to secure.

• Bake until golden brown on top, 20 to 25 minutes.

• Spoon 1 tablespoon of the cooled syrup on top of each purse as soon as you pull the pan from the oven. Serve warm.

• Purses can be made in advance. Reheat at 300°F until warmed through.

"I think of this dessert as our take on baklava." —*MIKE*

Making: Chocolate Nut Kataifi "Purses"

Cut the kataifi threads across the grain to create short fibers. Drizzle the melted butter over the top and toss gently but thoroughly with your fingers to ensure the kataifi is evenly coated.

Press the kaitaifi threads into "purses" on the bottom and sides of the muffin tin. Fill with the chocolate and nut mixture and pack more kataifi on top.

"You want a nice firm package. Don't be afraid to press these muffins down." —*KATREENA*

Coconut Macaroon Cake

Makes 10 servings

Macaroons are not just for Passover anymore. This decadent two-layer cake combines a rich vanilla base with a fluffy dome of coconut meringue.

FOR THE MERINGUE

- 3 egg whites, yolks reserved
- ½ cup sugar
- 1½ cups sweetened shredded coconut

• In a stand mixer fitted with a whisk attachment, beat the egg whites on medium speed until foamy.

• While the mixer whips the egg whites, gradually stream in the sugar. Increase to high speed and whip until you have stiff, glossy peaks.

• Transfer the meringue to a medium bowl. With a spatula, gently fold in the coconut until evenly mixed. Cover and refrigerate while you make the batter.

FOR THE BATTER

- Cooking spray or oil, for the pan
- 1 cup all-purpose flour
- 1½ teaspoons baking powder
- Pinch salt
- ½ cup (1 stick) butter, at room temperature, cut into 8 pieces
- 1 cup sugar
- 3 egg yolks
- 1 teaspoon vanilla extract
- ½ cup whole milk

• Oil and line a 9- or 10-inch springform pan (or round cake pan) with parchment paper. Then oil the top of the parchment. Preheat the oven to 325°F.

• In a medium bowl, stir together the flour, baking powder, and salt.

• Swap out the whisk in the stand mixer for a paddle attachment.

• Cream the butter and sugar until smooth and light in color. Add the egg yolks, one at a time, until incorporated. Add the vanilla.

• Add half of the milk, alternating with half of the flour mixture, and repeat with the remainder, mixing until just combined.

• Pour the batter into the prepared pan, tapping the pan on the counter to remove any air bubbles.

• Spread the coconut meringue on top until completely covered.

• Bake until a skewer inserted all the way into the cake (past the meringue) comes out clean, 35 to 40 minutes.

• Allow the cake to cool completely in the pan.

• Run a table knife around the edges of the pan and release the springform collar. Carefully transfer to a cake plate.

Making: Coconut Macaroon Cake

"If your recipe calls for both egg yolks and egg whites, beat the whites first so you needn't clean the mixer bowl!" *—KATREENA*

This is what a soft peak looks like, but it's not yet at the stiff peak stage we're looking for. Resist the urge to overwhip the egg whites, which will make them dry and sad, not glossy and lustrous.

Pavlova with Lemon Curd & Berries

Makes 6 servings

Don't be intimidated by the fancy name. A pavlova is just a meringue (egg whites whipped with sugar) that's named for a Russian ballerina. It's baked at a low temperature, so the outsides are crunchy and the inside is soft as a marshmallow. The lemon curd and unbaked meringue can be made the day before and refrigerated; the pavlovas are best served the same day they're baked. Plan on a half cup of berries per serving.

FOR THE MERINGUE

- Cooking spray or oil, for the pan
- 3 egg whites
- ½ cup plus 2 tablespoons granulated sugar
- ⅛ teaspoon kosher salt

• Oil a sheet pan with the spray. On a sheet of parchment paper taped to the counter, draw six 4-inch circles about 2 inches apart. Turn the paper over (so the ink does not mark the meringue) and lay it onto the prepared pan so that it sticks.

• Fill a medium saucepan halfway with water. Boil over high heat, then reduce to a simmer.

• Place a heat-resistant bowl on top of the saucepan to set up a double boiler (a metal bowl is ideal for heat absorption).

• Pour in the egg whites, sugar, and salt, whisking frequently until the mixture is 175°F, 8 to 10 minutes. Make sure to keep the mixture moving so that the egg whites don't cook on the bottom.

• Look for an opaque mixture that is foamy on top. Another test for doneness is to rub a small amount between your fingers; the mixture should be very warm and free of sugary grit.

• Transfer the egg white mixture to a stand mixer fitted with a whisk attachment. Whip on the highest speed until glossy and stiff, about 3 minutes.

• Preheat the oven to 200°F. Generously coat the top side of the parchment on the sheet pan with cooking spray.

• Fill a pastry bag (or a gallon-size plastic bag with one corner snipped off) and pipe 2 concentric rings of meringue onto each circle.

• Bake until the meringues have a slight marshmallow consistency—dry enough for a skin to develop, but still springing back when pressed, about 40 minutes.

• Turn off the oven, leaving the door ajar until the meringue has cooled.

• Carefully peel away the paper from the meringues. You may need a metal spatula.

FOR THE WHIPPED CREAM

- 1 cup heavy cream
- 2 tablespoons confectioners' sugar

• In a stand mixer with a whisk, beat the cream with the confectioners' sugar until stiff peaks form. Refrigerate until ready to serve.

FOR THE LEMON CURD

- ¾ cup granulated sugar
- Zest of 1 lemon
- 5 egg yolks
- ½ cup lemon juice (from 3 to 4 lemons)
- Pinch salt
- 6 tablespoons (¾ stick) butter, cubed

• Everything but the butter goes into a medium, nonreactive saucepan. Over medium heat, whisk the mixture constantly until it's smooth and the texture of pudding. This may take up to 10 minutes.

• Off the heat, add the cubed butter, whisking until it's no longer visible and the curd is smooth.

TO ASSEMBLE

• Center one meringue on a serving plate and fill with a few spoonfuls of lemon curd and a handful of berries. Top with whipped cream. Repeat with the remaining meringues, lemon curd, and whipped cream and serve immediately.

Making: Pavlova with Lemon Curd & Berries

"Crunchy meringue, rich, tart lemon curd, fresh berries, softly whipped cream—what more could you possibly want?"—*STEVE*

"I make this with the kids. It looks like a fancy dessert, but it's really not." —*STEVE*

In a Swiss meringue, egg whites and sugar are heated in a double boiler before being beaten in a stand mixer (as compared to the French meringue used in the Coconut Macaroon Cake, page 348, where no heat is applied). This leads to a plusher, denser, more stable meringue, reminiscent of Marshmallow Fluff.

Challah

"The aroma of fresh-baked bread is the best invitation." —*MIKE*

Challah

Makes 2 small loaves

When you think the dough is ready, let it proof for another fifteen minutes. This recipe calls for two cups of bread flour, which is very manageable in a home stand mixer. We like to form the dough into two smaller loaves—traditional for Shabbat—but feel free to make one large loaf if you like.

- ⅓ cup plus 2 tablespoons warm water
- 2¼ teaspoons instant dry yeast (1 envelope)
- 4 teaspoons honey
- 4 egg yolks
- 3 tablespoons olive oil, plus 1 teaspoon for oiling
- 2 cups bread flour
- 1½ teaspoons kosher salt (or 1⅛ teaspoons fine sea salt)

• In a small bowl, whisk the water with the yeast and 1 teaspoon of the honey. Let sit until the mixture becomes slightly foamy and/or bubbly, about 5 minutes.

• Lightly beat 3 of the egg yolks. In the bowl of a stand mixer, stir together the remaining 3 teaspoons of honey, the olive oil, and the 3 beaten egg yolks.

• In another small bowl, stir together the flour and salt.

• If your kitchen is cold, preheat the oven to its lowest temperature (about 170°F).

• Pour the yeast mixture on top of the egg yolk mixture. Then add the salted flour.

The dough should be smooth and elastic and pulling away from the sides of the bowl. Work on a completely dry surface so you won't need to add additional flour while shaping and rolling the dough.

- Using the mixer's dough hook attachment, mix and knead the dough for a total of 5 minutes in the following order:
  - 2 minutes on low (speed 2 on a KitchenAid)
  - 2 minutes on medium-low (speed 4)
  - 1 minute on low (speed 2)
- The dough should be smooth and pulling away from the sides of the bowl.
- If you are using the preheated oven to proof the dough, turn it off.
- Pour the 1 teaspoon of olive oil into a medium bowl.
- Gather the dough into a ball and coat it in the oil. Place plastic wrap directly onto the dough, followed by a towel.
- Proof in the preheated oven or another warm spot until doubled in size, about 2 hours.
- Cut the dough into 6 equal pieces and shape into smooth balls. Cover with plastic wrap and let rest for 15 minutes.
- Preheat the oven again to 170°F for the second rise.
- Line a sheet pan with oiled parchment paper.
- Form the balls, one at a time, into rope-shaped pieces with tapered ends, about 6½ inches long. Focus on a thickness of 1½ to 2 inches in the middle, then taper the ends.
- If the dough resists, cover and let rest for another 10 minutes.

(Continued on page 360)

Making: Challah

Roll out the ropes of dough by extending your arms outward—but try not to exert too much downward pressure. The idea is to shape the dough without forcing all the air out.

TO BRAID THE CHALLAH

- You'll need 3 dough ropes per loaf. Line up the ropes vertically about 1 inch apart.
- For each loaf, press together the skinny ends of the three dough ropes. Then carefully braid the strands together, tugging the dough lightly as you go.
- Turn the dough around so that the unbraided part is now the bottom half. Braid the same way. With the bottom of your palm, lightly press both ends together and tuck them underneath.
- If using the oven for the second rise, turn it off.
- Cover the braids with a towel or plastic wrap and proof until doubled in size, 1½ to 2 hours. The dough should be puffy and may even jiggle slightly when it's ready.
- Preheat the oven to 375°F.
- In a small bowl, whisk the remaining egg yolk with 1 tablespoon water. Brush the egg wash all over the loaves.
- Bake for 8 minutes, then rotate the pan from front to back. Bake for another 8 minutes. The challah should be deeply golden and reach an internal temperature of 200°F.
- Allow the bread to cool on the pan.
- To serve, slice or tear, preferably while still warm. Katreena advises, "You want to see strings on the inside of the dough."
- Challah freezes well, for up to 3 months. Wrap in plastic, then in foil. Remove the foil and plastic and reheat in a 350°F oven for 15 minutes.

Acknowledgments

Restaurants are a team sport and so is making cookbooks. We consider ourselves so fortunate to have been able to work with a group of future hall-of-famers for all four of our books:

- To the incomparable and visionary **Dorothy Kalins,** who fearlessly shaped and molded the ideas on these pages into something people would actually want to read, and whose trademark felt-tip pen magically cut through all the clutter to get right to the heart of the matter.

- To **Don Morris**, for designing a book that is as beautiful as it is (we hope) useful; for your generosity of spirit that inspires us to be better colleagues and collaborators; and for supplying pastries every morning to fuel our efforts.

- To **Mike Persico,** for your brilliant eye, trademark warmth, limitless patience, and pitch-perfect playlists—but mostly for your catlike ability to leap onto a kitchen island in a single bound to get those crucial overhead shots.

- To **Kim O'Donnel,** for tirelessly documenting the twists and turns of these recipes as they developed in real time; for converting pinches, spoonfuls, and handfuls into useful measurements; and for thoroughly testing the recipes so that our readers can cook them with confidence.

- To super-agent **David Black,** for your unqualified support and for creating the conditions under which we are somehow allowed to do this thing we love professionally.

- To our editor, **Sarah Kwak,** for supporting our vision and process, our publisher, **Deb Brody,** for her hearty enthusiasm, and to copy editor **Mark McCauslin** and production editorial manager **Rachel Meyers,** for their astute and welcome oversight.

- To **Beau Friedman, Natasha Sabanina, Joe Howard, Andrew Henshaw,** and **Katreena Kanney,** for making us look like we know what we're doing, keeping us in *mis en place,* and making it fun to come into work every day.

- To our **Zahav staff and customers,** for helping create the community we share together and for never being too shy to tell us when we can do better.

- To **Asima Ahmad,** for welcoming us into your home and allowing us to turn it into a test kitchen and photo studio, and for tolerating our siphoning off your Wi-Fi bandwidth.

- To **Shira Rudavsky,** for your love and support and for being one of the best, most fearless home cooks we know (aka a balabusta).

- To neighbors **Brian and Stephanie,** for graciously refusing to allow the fruits of our days-long photo shoots go to waste, and for inspiring the term "to neighbor"—*to responsibly dispose of excess food by giving it to someone nearby.*

ZAHAV HOME
Pantry Resources

Happily, since 2015, when we published our first book, *Zahav: A World of Israeli Cooking,* many of the once difficult-to-find ingredients we love have become staples on the shelves of good food markets everywhere: tehina, labneh, feta, pomegranate molasses, harissa, za'atar, preserved lemons, and many grains. Excellent purveyors now offer authentic herbs, spices, and sauces online. Many of our favorite companies are mission-based, often supporting small local farmers.

AL'ARD

This Pennsylvania-based company began with the goal of encouraging Palestinian farmers. Al'ard has grown as a trusted purveyor of high-quality Palestinian products such as olive oils, grains like freekah, the za'atar we love, and small buckets of little green olives. **alardproducts.com**

CURIO SPICE COMPANY

Claire Cheney's unique business began after she discovered her passion at our friend Ana Sortun's restaurants, Oleana and Sofra, in Cambridge, Massachusetts. As a company, Curio supports small farmers and organizations like World Central Kitchen. Their spices, intense and authentic, are composed of organic and fair-trade ingredients. We love Curio's pure, deep flavors, like smoked paprika, black lime, and cardamom. **curiospice.com**

LA BOÎTE

Lior Lev Sercarz, the Israeli-born, French-trained chef and world-class spice purveyor, has been our close friend and spice guru since the first days of Zahav. In fact, La Boîte sells a pretty adorable Zahav Mini-5 Spice Set, including baharat, mousa, shabazi, hawaij, and za'atar inspired by our first cookbook. It's a great starter spice kit. **laboiteny.com**

LOVENEH

Our friend (and neighbor) Dr. Emiliano Tatar and his family (page 29) make labneh and other cheeses at Merion Park Cheese Co. We love their fresh, creamy labneh, which is made from Armenian yogurt from Ervian Dairy in nearby Bucks County. **www.merionparkcheese.com**

KALUSTYAN'S

The answer to every cook's "Where will I find it?" dilemma, this treasure chest of spices and cooking ingredients now sprawls across several storefronts on New York's Lexington Avenue and offers products from India to, well, the whole world! **kalustyans.com**

NEW YORK SHUK

Ron and Leetal Arazi hand-craft Middle Eastern flavors into the flavor-forward spices and sauces we depend on when we're not making our own from scratch. Their harissa from a jar has saved many a dinner! **nyshuk.com**

SOOM

It's one of those hard-to-believe stories: From the day we opened Zahav in 2008, the three Zitelman sisters from Philadelphia who started Soom Tahini have been our major suppliers of that liquid gold! Now marketed across the country, and with chocolate and dark chocolate versions, Soom remains our go-to for tehina. **soomfoods.com**

Index

Index

G

H

Index

N

O

P

Index

Index

412

حبيبي
HABIBI